Taking Back Our Neighborhoods

Taking Back Our Neighborhoods

Building Communities That Work

Mary I. Wachter
with Cynthia Tinsley

Fairview Press   *Minneapolis*

Great things are not done by impulse,
but by a series of small things brought together.
—Vincent van Gogh

Published by Fairview Press, 2450 Riverside Avenue South, Minneapolis, MN 55454.

Library of Congress Cataloging-in-Publication Data

Wachter, Mary I., 1928–
    Taking back our neighborhoods : building communities that work / Mary I. Wachter.
        p.   cm.
    Includes bibliographical references and index.
    ISBN 1-57749-015-0 (hc : alk. paper)
    1. Community development—United States—Citizen participation. 2. Neighborhood—United States.   3. School facilities—Extended use—United States.   4. Community centers—United States.   5. Family services—United States.   6. Social problems—United States.
I. Tinsley, Cynthia. II. Title.
HN90.C6W27   1996
307.1'4—dc20   96-2936
                                                                                   CIP

First Printing: September 1996

Printed in the United States of America
00 99 98 97 96   7 6 5 4 3 2 1

Jacket design: Circus Design

Publisher's Note: Fairview Press publishes books and other materials related to the subjects of social and family issues. Its publications, including *Taking Back Our Neighborhoods*, do not necessarily reflect the philosophy of Fairview Hospital and Healthcare Services or their treatment programs.

For a free current catalog of Fairview Press titles, please call this toll-free number: 1-800-544-8207.

Contents

Acknowledgments

A first and most important acknowledgment goes to Wilfred J. Wachter, who helped conceive of and create the initial draft of this manuscript, for his contribution and support. One of his many accomplishments was his responsibility for the design and building of the first camera that went to the moon. This is just one example of his genius that was so inspiring to others. In a time when it was uncommon, he hired female engineers and mathematicians and had tremendous respect for women. Within the context of his inspiration and respect, this book came to fruition.

Art Wassnar, Ph.D., a clinical psychologist and good friend, was very patient in the early stages of preparation of this book. His sage advice and his assumed role as devil's advocate when appropriate were greatly appreciated.

Special thanks also to Jack Mumey, another long-suffering and patient supporter during the final stages of manuscript preparation. His commitment to work that makes a difference grants him the tremendously appreciated ability to give up his wife, quite literally, to this project.

Finally, but not least, our gratitude to Fairview Press for the opportunity to transform this idea into reality by allowing it to reach the public, where it belongs. Julie Smith and Ed Wedman, another special thanks to you.

Introduction

And it is characteristic of man that he alone has any sense of good and evil, of just and unjust, and the like, and the association of living beings who have this sense make a family and a state. —Aristotle

One has only to spend a half hour or so in city traffic to become thoroughly convinced that people have become self-centered. Only on rare occasions will one see another driver consider the consequences of his or her actions on the flow of traffic ahead or behind. Go ahead and try to change lanes. Watch people speed up, apparently oblivious to your signal, to reach the next stoplight before everyone else on the street. All other drivers appear single-mindedly intent upon getting themselves and themselves alone to their destinations—and safe arrival does not seem to be part of that intent.

It should be no surprise, then, to find similar evidence of such self-absorption in our communities and neighborhoods. Rarely will you find a homeowner picking up litter in the street while cleaning up her own lawn. The news media air reports almost daily, it seems, relating some story of one neighbor suing another over a loudly barking dog or raucous stereo.

Of course, the worst cases are those involving drive-by shootings or other gang-related crimes, burglaries, murders, rapes, beatings. Yet even these events are not as meaningful on a visceral level—until they happen in your neighborhood.

1

Reading about the tragic and senseless death of a child from abuse is not as disturbing as when it happens in the house down the street from your own.

The bad news (as if all this wasn't bad enough) is that these terrible events are happening more often in all neighborhoods. Why? Senator Daniel P. Moynihan (1986) suggested at least part of the cause when he wrote,

> From the wild Irish slums of the nineteenth-century eastern seaboard, to the riot-torn suburbs of Los Angeles, there is one unmistakable lesson in American history: a community that allows a large number of young men to grow up in broken families, dominated by women, never acquiring any stable relationships to male authority, never acquiring any set of rational expectations about the future—that community asks for and gets chaos, crime, violence, unrest, disorder—most particularly the furious, unrestrained lashing out at the whole social structure—that is not only expected; it is very near to inevitable. And it is richly deserved.

Single parents, of course, are not the cause of all the woes of our society. Young women as well as young men suffer the same effects of broken families, and these days men head many broken families. The erosion of the family unit as the source of values and positive role models for young people is the issue under scrutiny. We all share responsibility for that erosion as well as for the possibility of repairing the damage.

The purpose of this book is to offer tools for achieving a higher quality of life for everyone willing to make that possible. This higher quality of life includes better and higher education, affordable daycare, skills for better-paying jobs, free healthcare, and effective parenting skills. These issues are not just someone else's problem. The objective is to suggest a plan for people to take more shared responsibility for reclaiming their neighborhoods by making them pleasant, safe, and vital places in which to live with pride. Therefore, this book will not single out broken families or any other single group for embarrassment or blame. Rather, the information and proposals apply to two-parent families, singles, seniors, and other family combinations.

A new concept called the neighborhood campus and shared responsibility form the core of the proposed plan. Execution of the plan involves following the village model. You (yes, you) have the ability to revitalize your neighborhood, stabilize the family unit, attack poverty and violence, resurrect the dream of a happy childhood for young people, and elevate the quality of education available. These things you can do without spending more money. To provide even more tools to accomplish this task, information and ideas are included to allow you to make the transition from reality as it exists to what probably sounds like a utopian dream right now.

The process requires work, and some of that work begins now. There are some definitions to cover, and statistics are necessary to see the true condition of what you will be sculpting and molding in your role as a social artist. To help make the work more enjoyable and to inspire you, also included are some good stories of successful examples of this plan and others.

To clarify the meaning of some of the concepts used in this plan, following are a few short, simple definitions.

The Change Process and the Change Agent

To make reclaiming your neighborhood a reality and not just a great idea, change must take place. The process of change is a framework for discussion of the ultimate goal. A change agent, or social artist, studies a situation, monitors and facilitates the various stages of change required to reach the desired goal, and continually reinforces the vision that inspires the change. To be a proficient and effective change agent, one must be ready for these various stages of implementing a plan involving a group of people. Many of the concepts discussed are drawn from the areas of business, psychology, education, and sociology.

Bringing about change is similar whether at the personal, family, neighborhood, city, national, or global levels. Appendix C is dedicated to further discussion of the change process, planning the process, and the role of the change agent. This appendix, as well as Appendices A and B, are consolidated and separated for your use at any time while reading this book or pursuing your plan. A number of resources for additional information are included in Appendix C.

A New Definition of Family

Based on historical and sociological research, a primary premise of this book is that a stable family unit and village system is the foundation of civilization. When the family breaks down, neighborhoods decay and society deteriorates. Crime, violence, and finally chaos, the state we are fast approaching, replace law and order. This approach may appear simplistic on the surface, but it is profound and represents a starting place from which to begin making changes.

These days the word "family" doesn't mean quite the same thing as it used to mean. Television and other forms of social conditioning have worked to present an ideal image of the family as two opposite-sex parents, white, middle class, with two-point-whatever children. That image and definition simply do not work anymore.

One basic, applicable definition includes the following characteristics common to all family forms:

> First, the family consists of a group of people who are in some way related to one another. Second, its members live together for long periods. Third, the adults in the group assume responsibility for any offspring. And fourth, the members of the family form an economic unit—often for producing goods and services (as when all members share

agricultural tasks) and always for consuming goods and services (such as food or housing). We may say, then, that the *family* is a relatively permanent group of people related by ancestry, marriage, or adoption, who live together, form an economic unit, and take care of their young (Robertson 1987, 348).

The reality today is that increasing numbers of relationships include the elements of this definition but do not fit the outdated ideal image of family. There were almost 15 million single-parent households in 1993; about 12 million were headed by females, the other 3 million by males with no spouse present. Many single-parent families combine their resources, children, and households to survive. Gay and lesbian couples are struggling to find their legal place in our society, and committed but unmarried couples raising families are no longer unusual—more than 3 million of them in 1993. More than 2 million children live with grandparents or other relatives (Aburdene and Naisbitt 1992; Wright 1996). Such non-traditional relationships can still be called families. There may be a number of different situations in your personal experience and neighborhood that also fit the definition but not the old ideal.

The Village Model

Webster's unabridged dictionary cites one of the definitions of a village as "a relatively small group of people organized chiefly in families that constitutes a distinct social unit and usually forms a community." Aristotle wrote, "The association which is naturally formed for the satisfaction of daily needs is the household. . . . The primary association of several households, on a basis other than everyday needs, is the village" (MacKendrick 1952, 369). The concept of village implies a relationship or familiarity between the members living within the community. Usually our neighborhoods do not incorporate this relationship and familiarity because we are usually thrown together by circumstances. In most cases, we do not choose our neighborhoods based on family ties or close friendships with others living in them. However, this turn of fate does not preclude the possibility for developing a village-like environment in our existing communities.

If you saw the movie *Witness* with Harrison Ford, Kelly McGillis, and Alexander Godunov, think of the barn-raising scene. The entire community combined their time and energy to build a barn for a newlywed couple. The men supplied the labor while the women provided cool drinks and food. This shared effort reduced a daunting and lengthy project to a simple, one- or two-day effort rewarded with social interaction. The flavor of the village concept in this example, rather than the particular roles of the sexes, defines the village model for the purposes of this book.

The Neighborhood Campus

You can take back your neighborhoods and build communities that work by using facilities, services, and organizations already in place and operating. This plan proposes the expanded utilization of public elementary schools in the neighborhood, which would become the neighborhood campuses.

The neighborhood campus offers the possibility of free centers for

> Daycare
> Parent training
> After-school arts and recreation
> Health and welfare
> Senior citizens
> Twenty-four hour crisis intervention

Because the neighborhood campus represents the vision of transformed neighborhoods and is the core of this book, chapters are devoted to the concept as well as each of the centers.

Sometimes, almost always, people greet new ideas with cynicism and mistrust. Often great ideas fail because they are not supported by effective action. In realizing the dream of taking back your neighborhoods, belief and desire are valuable only if backed by commitment and persistence. Facing and overcoming barriers like indifference, resistance, and others natural to any change process is possible, if not easy. Here's help!

Start by asking some questions of yourself and others. Don't try to find immediate answers to these questions. Jot them down or remind yourself of them for several days or weeks as you go about your normal business.

What is the definition of a "good" neighborhood? What makes a good neighborhood? How and why did we lose control over the direction of our neighborhood? How can we take our neighborhood back and make it a better place to live?

What values seem apparent in the current state of our neighborhood? Do we have a set of values? Are the apparent values the values we want? What kind of life do we want for our families tomorrow? What can each of us do? What can we do as a community?

Change is not possible until we can see the need for change. The first step is to open your eyes to what is real in your neighborhood today. Sometimes, even though reality should be obvious, it can also be frightening or discouraging, and people may try to ignore it by pretending things really aren't that way at all. Portions of this book will examine the true state of the family, the neighborhood, and the community as well as the state of those who make up those groups. The rest of the book is devoted to the neighborhood campus, each center at the campus, and examples of how the campus concept has worked for others. Appendix A contains step-by-step suggestions for establishing your neighborhood campus, and Appendix B offers a sample curriculum to use.

Let's go take your neighborhood back!

1

The Evolution of Our Communities

Action research is a form of collective self-reflective enquiry undertaken by participants in social situations in order to improve the rationality and justice of their own social or educational practices, as well as their understanding of these practices and the situations in which these practices are carried out.
Groups of participants can be teachers, students, principals, parents and other community members—any group with a shared concern.
— Stephen Kemmis and Robin McTaggart

One method of bringing about change on a large scale, as in an organization or a community, involves the use of action research. This method was first given its name by Kurt Lewin, a social scientist who led action research studies during World War II. Action research is a process of social change, rather than a set of techniques or some specific knowledge to be applied to particular problems (McLennan 1980). What this approach means for you, the change agent, is that you can change your neighborhood with your existing level of skills and education. You begin with the current problems as you and your community members define them, and take action to resolve them. The only requirement is that you must be will-

9

ing to observe and analyze your environment with no illusions. The research part is important throughout the process, including the research necessary to find ways to move into action.

The place to begin your action research is with some background information about your community. This chapter and the following two chapters will examine some historical facts and current information about some of the problems shared by or affecting all of us. For areas you and your neighbors want to address specifically, you can continue your own research and action as necessary. Additional information and resources are available in Appendix C to guide you at that stage.

The first question is, what is the background of our communities and why have they evolved in the ways they have?

The pattern for the development of communities in the United States originated with western European civilization and the agricultural society that developed there. During the Middle Ages, stability of village life depended upon the strength of the family, which in turn depended upon farming for survival. The structure of medieval communities developed as a result of constant conflict between families over power and land—power to control the land and resources necessary to produce food for growing families.

As families grew, several generations shared the family lands. When outside threats became more unacceptable than an alliance with another family, the families combined resources for mutual protection. For example, one family might have lived in a hamlet, but lacked protection from marauding bands of outlaws that roamed across the land. For the sake of security, they formed an alliance with several neighboring families and built a walled town on top of the nearest high hill.

This stronger sense of security enabled these small town societies to enforce their rules, because it reinforced the need of the residents to have a sense of belonging. As one of the stronger forms of punishment for disobeying the rules, the townspeople would ostracize or even expel the offender. He

10

either became a hermit or an outlaw. His family, if he had one, accompanied him. They had no choice. They were outside of the laws and rules of their society (Mumford 1934, 41). In this way, the towns could maintain the stability of the family and the group.

Families found that when they lived together and shared responsibility for managing and protecting their lands and town, they had more time to care for their crops and domesticated animals. They were able to cultivate cottage industries such as weaving cloth, constructing houses, and building furniture. More leisure time allowed the residents to hold trade fairs and farmers' markets, watch and participate in sports, and pursue the arts.

As the town prospered, other families joined the alliance and the town became a city. Since specialized skills were needed to build and maintain a city, extended families developed different skills. Perhaps one family developed skills in blacksmithing, another trained their young members in stone cutting or masonry, while still another made wooden furniture. Commerce began to flourish because these families no longer had the time to do subsistence farming. They relied upon bartering and trade to obtain the necessities for living.

As the city grew, neighborhoods formed around focal points with which residents could identify. A geographical feature like a hill, valley, or river, or a prominent building such as a cathedral or the town hall served as a neighborhood identification. Families in the same trade tended to live in the same neighborhood. Craftsmen and artisans formed trade guilds, the predecessors of present-day unions, as the number of families in each trade grew. To learn an occupation, young men entered a trade as apprentices to an experienced tradesman.

Some workers were skilled in trades that usually meant employment for temporary jobs, such as building a cathedral. When they completed a job, these tradesmen and their families moved on to another town. Other than these workers, however, families rarely left their neighborhoods. As those neighborhoods grew, merchants moved into permanent stores. Trade became more elaborate and money became a medium of exchange.

Often, members of the clergy were the only literate people. Towns also grew up near monasteries, and the monks were responsible for the first written forms of communication between towns. The monks traveled throughout Europe visiting different monasteries and exchanging scrolls. Much of the history of different regions, previously communicated through local stories and songs, was first written on scrolls by the monks. Later, as trade became more complicated, the need for accurate record keeping provided an incentive for a more developed and widespread system of writing.

Agricultural societies tend to be relatively wealthy and settled. These characteristics allow for investment of surplus resources in cultural artifacts—artwork such as paintings and sculptures, buildings and monuments, palaces and stadiums, for example. This type of society also allows for the development of institutions such as religion, economic order, political order, and education. An institution is "a stable cluster of values, norms, statuses, roles, and groups that develops around a basic social need" (Robertson 1987, 93). These institutions were often the source of social problems when they failed, and still are when they fail now. A failure in the economy that results in unemployment, for instance, can create social problems. Institutions are also notoriously resistant to change.

As these European societies developed and became more sophisticated, they began to explore the world in search of more land and more riches to feed their need for power. Eventually, as we know, these explorers ended up over here in America. When they came, they brought all the values and norms and cultures characteristic of their social structure.

The next stage in social development in this whirlwind summary is the Industrial Revolution. With its beginning approximately two hundred years ago in Great Britain, this period was "the rapid transition from a predominantly agrarian to a predominantly industrial economy—the starting point of a new period in world history" (Barraclough 1984).

America grew up primarily during this period of industrialization, and so our society developed as one relying for its substance primarily on mechanized production. Industrialism means a few people can feed the majority, and allows for the rapid growth of populations to very large numbers. Societies become very urbanized, populations congregate in cities where the jobs are, and social life takes place in groups other than the family or neighborhood.

Robertson (1987, 106) sums up some of the effects of industrialism on institutions as follows:

> The economy, of course, becomes vast, complex, and pervasive in its effects on the whole society. The family loses many of its earlier functions; it is no longer a unit of economic production, nor does it have the main responsibility for the education of the young. The influence of religion as an unquestioned source of moral authority also shrinks, for people no longer share similar life experiences and consequently hold many different and competing values and beliefs. Science, however, emerges as a new and important social institution, because technological innovation depends on the growth and refinement of scientific knowledge. Similarly, education becomes a distinct institution: an industrial society requires mass literacy, and for the first time formal education becomes compulsory for the many rather than a luxury for the few. Other institutions, such as law, sport, medicine, and the military, grow more elaborate.

So while industrialism makes possible wonderful material conveniences and a more diverse culture, its effectiveness is based on exploitation of the environment—which, of course, brings up a bunch of new problems. We have to contend with pollution, depletion of natural resources, loss of entire species of plants and animals. Industrialism devastates traditional values and communities and disrupts kinship systems. People become anonymous in the rapidly growing cities. The extraordinarily rapid rate of social change continually attacks the social structure.

Sound familiar?

Now, just when you may think you've caught up and can at least deal with the evolution of our communities so far, there is another stage to consider. The next development is the postindustrial society. Even as few as ten years ago this next sociocultural development was considered a logical but uncertain prediction. With the breathtaking advancements in information and computer technology, seemingly in mere weeks rather than years, the prediction has come true.

We don't really *do* things anymore, or at least we don't have to do things the way our ancestors did. We're becoming a "virtual society," in which communication and interaction and a great many jobs take place in a make-believe computer-generated world. Some of us are still not comfortable with the thought of virtual payment for our services, let alone virtual banking, virtual reality, and virtual sex.

In such a society, education and science are vastly elevated, and mastery of them becomes the key to success and status. Those who have education and technical knowledge, who can control information and make decisions, are those who emerge in positions of control. Mental rather than physical effort is the hallmark of ever increasing numbers of jobs. "As a result of the size, mobility, educational level, and widely differing life experiences of their populations, postindustrial societies have relatively varied, tolerant, and heterogeneous cultures. Subcultures and 'lifestyles' proliferate, and people become deeply concerned with individual self-fulfillment" (Robertson 1987, 108).

In such a society, it is easy to forget that we are still dependent upon the ecosystem of our planet. We are at the mercy of catastrophes that might disrupt the global network we are creating. Would we know how to produce our own food and build our own shelters if some disaster interrupted the flow of information upon which we increasingly rely?

With issues such as these, every day we face challenges to our sense of self, worth, and belonging. We can't even count on knowing right from wrong all the time anymore. The advent of genetic engineering has brought many benefits— improved food sources, for example. However, that and other developments raise many ethical and moral issues with which we are unequipped to cope. For example, how far should we go with the potential of genetic engineering? Should we engineer our kids? Parents have to consider the option of locking out access to certain choices on their televisions and computers if there are children in the house. They can only hope that the parents of their children's friends do the same.

The questions are too innumerable to scroll through in this book (even our language is changing). The result, however, is that we are struggling to keep up, and struggling to manage in a society where significant changes take place constantly. We do not have time to recover and regain our bearings in relation to our environment between changes. We don't know where we fit in this world much of the time; our roles, our jobs, and our knowledge are constantly at risk.

Identifying and clarifying basic issues such as family values is increasingly difficult. As mentioned in the introduction, we even have to redefine family. We are struggling to find a sense of belonging somewhere, and we're not sure we're not lost.

Now that you're reeling from this crash course in our community evolution, let's look at some of the problems that are convincing arguments that, indeed, we may have lost our way. Do remember, however, that we cannot only find our way again, but also choose to forge a new and better way.

2
Our Neighborhoods Today
Part I: Daycare, Education, and Seniors

Perhaps hope lies less in the direction of grand theories than in the capacity to see . . . to assume what the Buddhists call beginner's mind. And to see what exists freshly and without prejudice clears the path for seeing what might exist in the future, or what is possible. —Susan Griffin

One of the most difficult parts of change is accepting the present reality, harsh as it may be, of what must become different. Recognizing the truth about the evolution of your neighborhood to its present state may cause you to feel frustration, anger, sadness, guilt, hopelessness—all at once or in any combination. Fully accepting the state of your community may be difficult because no matter what that state is, it is comfortable. It is comfortable because it is familiar, and as always it is easier to keep what we know than to face the unknown future that change brings. Putting up with what's not working and talking about the problems (complaining about them, if we're truthful) is far more comfortable than doing something about them.

However, if you do look at your neighborhood with a fresh eye and without prejudice and you see problems with which you are no longer willing to live, then you have reached a moment of choice. One choice is to leave. Another is to stay and try to tolerate the situation. Yet another choice is to say emphatically, "This is my home and I will make it a place where I am happy and proud to live." Before you can choose, however, you must accept what is so.

In this and the next chapter, you will read statistics and information about your society in general. Again, these facts and figures may not reflect the condition of your particular community or situation. They represent communities all over the country. What we all have in common is that this data indicates trends that will eventually affect us all if left unchecked.

With the quality of life in mind for all of us, but especially for children, let's see what trends we need to check.

Daycare

"If children are denied love and nurturing before the age of two, their growth will be retarded both mentally and physically. Infants who are not touched or talked to will die rather than eat, which sadly demonstrates that the need to belong is the most basic of human needs" (Restak 1986, 34). The brain is basically developed by the time a child starts preschool. A person's life script is written by the age of four or five, before he or she can filter out undesirable influences. In an interview with Cynthia Tinsley in July 1996, author and psychotherapist Jack Mumey defined life script as "the way a person will deal with life situations sociologically, psychologically, and physiologically." Mumey further said that the life script is based on what a child is exposed to in his or her environment from birth to age five. In other words, a child develops a pattern for living based on the role models and circumstances present during those earliest years. Rewriting that script is always possible, but often only after many confusing and traumatic experiences or many hours of therapy.

Patricia Aburdene and John Naisbitt (1992, 260) tell us that childcare workers share low morale and education. The field also has a high rate of turnover of about 40 percent a year. This turnover rate, which means that most daycare teachers change jobs after less than a year (Gordon 1989), is largely caused by inadequate pay. We may be unrealistic to expect that daycare workers with low morale who are poorly paid will be motivated to provide that all-important love and nurturing during those early years. Yet many of these under-valued people do try to meet this unrealistic expectation. A study by the *Pittsburgh Post-Gazette* revealed that most providers care about children and want to do the best they can for them. However, daycare is underfunded, undertrained, disrespected, both overregulated and underassisted, and criticized for not being better.

Mackenzie Carpenter and Sally Kalson, who shared that information in their article "Daycare: The 'quiet' crisis scream-ing for relief" in the July 7, 1996, Denver *Rocky Mountain News*, also said: "What children need from daycare is warm nurturing attention that is physically safe, emotionally secure and devel-opmentally appropriate. What they get, in too many cases, is a place where they're lost in a crowd, spoken to harshly, parked in front of a TV set all day or devastated when the care-giver they love suddenly leaves." A study by the National Institute of Child Health and Development found that the quality of daycare could significantly affect the emotional security of infants. If a parent has poor parenting skills, poor-quality daycare is harmful to that security. However, high-quality daycare can increase the security of children whose parents had the worst relationships with them.

Thirty-six percent of working men in 1990 (24 million) were fathers of children under the age of eighteen, half of whom had children under six years old. In 1989, the Census Bureau estimated US births in 1990 would be 3.7 million; the actual number was 4.2 million. That was the most births in one year since the late baby boom year of 1961. Most of these were not births to unwed teens, either. Most women with children under the age of six work (53 percent), and single parents numbering almost 8 million are raising 30 percent of all children. No wonder daycare is the seventh-fastest-growing industry in America, according to the US Department of Labor.

Although many businesses are waking up to the need to provide daycare for their workers, most fail to do so, despite these figures. Small businesses employ the majority of working parents at the lowest pay scale with a minimum of benefits. Parents not only do not receive the option of daycare as a benefit, but also do not have the income to pay for good daycare (US Dept. of Labor 1983). The average family spends about $500 a month for daycare. Put another way, a middle-class family spends around 10 percent of its income for daycare, while a poor family—even with lower fees—spends as much as a quarter of its income.

Furthermore, businesses lose in the long run by not offering daycare benefits. The numbers indicate that more than 90 percent of children have working parents. When a child is ill or needs medical and dental checkups, one of those parents must take time from work. Caring for their children is a constant source of anxiety for these working parents. This anxiety takes its toll in stress not only on their performance on the job, but also on their families.

In recent years, there has been a disturbing increase in the number of reports of child abuse and negligence in some daycare operations. Parents are considering the need to videotape baby-sitters in their homes. These may be isolated incidents, yet they remind us how important it is that parents know what to look for in a daycare provider. Only 15 percent of children under age five are enrolled in certified licensed centers with high standards and well-paid, qualified teachers.

Something must change for our children to have their best chance to develop healthy, happy, active bodies and minds during those critical early years. Parents will—must—continue to work. They must have access to high-quality, safe, affordable daycare, not just for their peace of mind and convenience, but for all of us. Those children are our future coworkers, neighbors, employers, and political leaders. Who will we want to sit next to or vote for twenty or thirty years from now—the person who started out with a well-written life script, or the one who did not?

Education

A great deal of information is available about educational curricula, problems, possible solutions, and resources. Here we can look briefly at only a few of the problem areas that we can address with this plan to take back our neighborhoods—illiteracy, sex education, and parent education.

In September 1993, the US Department of Education released the most detailed portrait ever available on the condition of literacy in America. According to that National Adult Literacy Survey, 21 to 23 percent (40 to 44 million) adults are at level 1 literacy. That means almost one adult of every four is functionally illiterate, defined as unable to use reading, writing, and computational skills in everyday life situations. Another 25 to 28 percent, 50 million adults, are classified just one level higher on the literacy scale. Almost half the adult population, then, is unable or barely able to read, write, and do basic arithmetic. Unfortunately, another truth we must face is that a heavy concentration of our fellow Americans who are literacy-challenged are among the poor and those dependent on public financial support.

Ironically, in 1993 we were spending about $14, 667 a year for each person in prison. We were spending less than $6,000 per child in public elementary and secondary schools (Wright 1996). This is one of those present harsh realities we must tell the truth about before we can start making changes. We may think and say our priority is to support high-quality public education, but the reality is that we're supporting criminals and the prison system better.

If you're reading this book, you're literate. So why should you care about illiteracy? For one thing, approximately 15 million adults holding jobs today are functionally illiterate. The American Council of Life Insurance reports that three-quarters of the Fortune 500 companies provide some level of remedial training for their workers. Business losses attributable to basic skill deficiencies run into hundreds of millions of dollars because of low productivity, errors, and accidents, according to the Literacy at Work study by the Northeast-Midwest Institute and The Center for Regional Policy (*Facts* 1996). We consumers, therefore, indirectly pay the cost of correcting illiteracy through the cost of goods and services we purchase from these companies. That's in addition to what we already pay to support public education, or private education if your children are in private schools.

There is yet another reason you should care about illiteracy. All the sex education in the world won't be effective in preventing unwanted pregnancies or the spread of disease if people can't read and understand even the instructions for the proper use of a condom. There is a correct way to put on a condom to minimize accidental tearing or rupture, for example. Another very valuable piece of information to look for on the package is whether the condom is lubricated with a spermicide containing nonoxynol-9. Nonoxynol-9 is important because it can kill the HIV virus, which otherwise can pass through animal membrane condoms. People need to be able to recognize that name. Failure to read and comprehend this information can result in unwanted pregnancy as well as the spread of disease. Taking the process back yet another step, people must be able to understand the importance of this knowledge in the first place. At the very least, an unwanted pregnancy or one more case of HIV infection affects the individual, his or her child or children, and all the rest of us in our tax and healthcare bills.

In 1992, nearly three-quarters of all teenagers between ages fifteen and nineteen who gave birth were unwed mothers (Wright 1996, 303–4). Many of these young women didn't have the time to mature into adults before becoming pregnant, much less develop the skills needed to manage a family and provide love and nurturing to a child.

Teenage boys who become fathers suffer from the same obstacles. As late as 1983, very little information was available about teenage fathers. In 1992, Karen Gravelle and Leslie Peterson interviewed thirteen teenage fathers. The resulting book explores the feelings and experiences of these young men. While girls tend to think of sex and love together, teenage boys do not. Some of the fathers refused to have anything to do with their children. They lacked role models for effective fathering because their own fathers were not present in their homes. The rest of the young men accepted varying degrees of responsibility for being fathers. Because of their immaturity, maintaining a good relationship with the mother of their children was difficult for the boys. Without the time and opportunity to learn job skills and complete a proper education, these young fathers felt considerable stress to provide for their families emotionally and financially.

Too often, children lack the education they need to understand their sexual and emotional makeup. Positive role models could and do help compensate for educational deficiencies, but even those are often missing. The threat of AIDS and the sex education available in our schools have failed to affect the increasing numbers of young unwed parents, especially among the poor.

Teenagers are trying sex at younger ages. "Although the number of very young teenagers (thirteen- and fourteen-year-olds) having sex remains very low, sexual activity continues to increase among teenagers of all ages. In 1987, for example, 21 percent of sixteen-year-old girls said they had had intercourse, compared with 9 percent in 1972. . . . Among boys, 41 percent of sixteen-year-olds had had sex in 1987, compared with 30 percent respectively in 1972" (Wright 1996, 317).

Furthermore, a 1992 report indicated that 19 percent of American high school students have had four or more sex partners. Having multiple sex partners puts them at high risk for contracting AIDS as well as other sexually transmitted diseases.

Today forty-seven states require some sort of sex education and all fifty have AIDS education. But students receive mixed messages from their parents, schools, and communities. Some schools make condoms readily available, while others tell teens to just wait.

Considering again that life scripts are written before the age of five, babies born to children may be at a disadvantage during those first formative years. While their teenage parent or parents struggle to cope, the babies may be exposed to confusion, anxiety, and perhaps poverty and alienation. The pattern is perpetuated in this way. The way to break the pattern is to improve the quality of sex education and increase positive role models available to young people. Which brings up that same difficulty in making changes—belief versus reality.

The issue of sex education is a subject that many attempt to turn into a moral and ethical debate. At that level, the issue is one that individuals and families must decide. Despite religious and moral beliefs, however, there are some facts with which we simply have to deal. Father Andrew M. Greeley, novelist and staff member at the University of Chicago's National Opinion Research Center, said, "When kids hit their teenage years and their hormones are surging, an ad[vertisement] is not going to stop them from experimenting. What *does* have an impact is their parents—not what they say but the example they set." (Father Greeley was responding to a question about the effectiveness of advertising encouraging adolescent girls to postpone sex, printed in Walter Scott's "Personality Profile" in the July 14, 1996, issue of *Parade* magazine.) This natural combustion of hormones mixed with curiosity is not right or wrong; it is simply human. Put those two traits together and our personal opinions about sex education become mostly irrelevant. We cannot reasonably expect to completely eliminate inappropriate sexual activity, but we can reasonably expect to provide complete and accurate information about sex and the potential consequences of intercourse. Furthermore, rather than judge whether the expecting unwed teen was right or wrong, we can offer our best efforts to help her or him raise the healthiest, best-adjusted child possible.

So we come to parent training and education. There are many young parents out there who don't know how to parent, and there are many older parents out there who don't know how, either. First Lady Hillary Rodham Clinton (1996) said in her book, *It Takes a Village:*

> Like many women, I had read books when I was pregnant—wonderful books filled with dos and don'ts about what babies need in the first months and years to ensure the proper development of their bodies, brains, and characters. But as every parent soon discovers, grasping concepts in the abstract and knowing what to do with the baby in your hands are two radically different things. Babies don't come with handy sets of instructions.

Way back when in the good old days, new parents learned what to with the baby from their parents and grandparents, who usually lived with or very near them. Another reality we have to face is that this type of built-in family mentoring will probably not return as the norm in our present society. New parents need the training in nurturing and caring for their children that they no longer receive from an extended family. We have to devise some substitute system to teach new parents what to do, especially those without benefit of spouse, knowledgeable parents, thorough prenatal and postnatal education, or sufficient financial resources. This system should include

information about physiological and psychological consequences of the expectant mother's health and behavior on her
developing baby. Knowledge about the effect of either or both
parents' behavior on the development of the child after birth is
equally important.

Humans have the ability to think and understand at a higher level than any other animal, yet we only develop about 15
percent of our brains. The more children learn, the more wonder they find in the world around them and the more they
want to know. Their minds are curious about everything in the
world. Once humans discover that learning is a joy, they will
continue to learn until they die.

Our children learn through imitating their parents. A baby
will become completely absorbed by the expressions on people's faces or fascinated by clasping a finger. The sound of their
mother's and father's voices captivates babies. If the parent
smiles, the baby smiles. If they talk to him and cuddle and love
him, the baby will be comfortable with talking and cuddling
and loving. All parents should be aware of these pieces of
information, especially new parents.

Studies show that children living in single-parent families
often experience socioeconomic effects that endure for a lifetime, such as breakups of their own marriages, fewer years of
formal education, and juvenile delinquency (Moynihan 1986,
23–24). Again, this trend exists and we have to accept it as a
fact of our society. Further, we have to accept that there will
continue to be single-parent families for a very long time. The
trick is not to make all those families change miraculously to
fit the old two-parent, perfectly adjusted family ideal. Rather,
we can provide training and resources so those single parents
learn how to ensure that their children do not suffer because of
family structure, or economic status, or any other condition
dictated by fate or circumstance.

In our nation, there are more than three hundred federally
funded agencies giving aid to children and families, but they
are faltering (Pines 1982, 131). In towns and cities all over the

country, mayors boast about new programs to improve their public schools and decaying neighborhoods, and to fight violence and crime in their communities. Many of these programs flounder because they fail to attack the problems as a system of interrelated parts.

Clearly, we cannot include a complete analysis of education here. You can identify and research problems specific to your neighborhood, and there are many excellent resources to help you. We'll just close this section with a quotation borrowed from Benjamin Disraeli (1874) and applied to our country: "Upon the education of the people of this country the fate of this country depends."

Seniors

The aged have some distinct problems that are universal in their group, yet seniors can still be important players in the effort to reclaim our neighborhoods. Health concerns associated with the gradual deterioration of the body, consequent high medical expenses, work and retirement, isolation, and fear of becoming dependent are among these problems.

While the overall economic status of the aging has improved over the last decade, 7.9 percent of elderly men and 15.5 percent of elderly women were poor in 1991. At that time, the poverty threshold was $6,532 for a person sixty-five years and older living alone and $8,241 for a married couple with a householder sixty-five years or older. The Bureau of the Census, National Institute on Aging, published the report containing these figures and most of those following in 1993. That report also stated, "There is a significant difference in the likelihood of being poor depending on whether an elderly person lives in a family setting, or lives alone. Only 5.1 percent of elderly married couples were poor in 1991. This contrasts sharply with the elderly who lived alone: 17.6 percent of elderly men and 26.6 percent of elderly women who lived alone were poor in 1991."

In 1992, just over 32 million of the United States population were sixty-five or older. Of this group 9.5 million lived alone, 16.5 million lived with a spouse, and the rest lived with other relatives or nonrelatives. Eight out of ten of those living alone were women. The proportions of the elderly living alone changed significantly with age: about one-third of women between sixty-five and seventy-four years lived alone compared to over half aged eighty-five and over. For men, 13 percent of those aged sixty-five to seventy-four years lived alone, compared to 32 percent eighty-five years and older. Most of the elderly women who lived alone were widows.

Contrary to popular belief that a large portion of the aged live in nursing homes, only 5.1 percent actually reside in those facilities. However, the elderly do account for 90 percent of residents of nursing homes. Most of those residents were ninety-five years or older, but still about half of people in that age group live in the community.

Care of the elderly presents some problems for the younger generations. "More than one in five working adults provides some care for an elderly relative, usually a parent or parent-in-law, and loses an average of one week's work a year," according to social-welfare researcher Andrew Scharlach at the University of California, Berkeley. The average age of caregivers is fifty years old" (Aburdene 1992, 261). Three-quarters of these caregivers are women, and nearly 2 million women care for kids and parents at the same time. More than half of those caring for elderly relatives work outside the home, and almost 40 percent are still raising their own children. Elder care is a crucial need now, and will reach crisis proportions in the next few years.

The significance of this information is that we can still benefit from the knowledge of these elders even if they're not members of our own families. At the same time, we have the opportunity to help alleviate some of their problems and concerns. Seniors, like our children, represent a great untapped reservoir of potential resources to help us sculpt our future.

However, there is another potential set of aging-related problems looming in the future, and those problems will come of age with the 78 million Americans born between 1946 and 1964. This group, the baby boomers, are caring for their parents (and even, in some cases, their grandparents) right along with their own children (and sometimes grandchildren). They are also creating some problems for their own care as they reach their golden years. The baby boomers are so influential that their aging has its own name: the graying of America.

> The United States is in the midst of a profound change in the age structure of its population, one that will affect virtually every area of national life over the next half century. . . . At present [1987] there are over 28 million aged Americans, representing just over one in ten of the population. By the year 2030 there will be over 50 million aged people representing approximately one in every five Americans. Conversely, the proportion of the population that is under sixteen has [shrunk] to 22 percent today [1987] (Robertson 1987, 340).

In a recent article, Paula Spencer (1996) cited Cheryl Russell, author of *The Master Trend: How the Baby Boom Generation Is Reshaping America*, when she wrote: "Since its origin in the postwar years, the baby boom generation has grown up indulged, individualistic, independent and rebellious." Spencer also quoted from *The Sibling Society* by Richard Bly, who wrote, "People don't bother to grow up, and we are all fish swimming in a tank of half-adults." Bly worries, Spencer continued, that today's teens will have no desire to act adult themselves because they see so many regressed adults in an eternally youthful culture. Those adults provide no role models to show adolescents the way to responsible adulthood. Finally, Spencer wrote that "boomers are notoriously poor savers, facing increasing health costs, few pensions, an uncertain Social Security system and longer life expectancies than their parents had when they retired at sixty-five. What's more, most boomers have yet to face such common calamities as disease or chronic illness or the death of one's parents. What a country whose majority is over age fifty will really be like is still anyone's guess."

Well. The message seems clear enough. We need to deal with the present aging population, and we had better be looking at some solutions that will carry the boomers through the next decades as they experience the aging process.

One other quality of the baby boomers is their influence on American society by virtue of sheer numbers. They will be determining the allocation of resources among the different age groups well into the next century. Our challenge is to make sure that no major age stratum is denied a fair share of those resources (Robertson 1987, 341).

3
Our Neighborhoods Today
Part II: Poverty and Welfare, Crime, Substance Abuse and Mental Illness

Many people say to me, "I'd like to learn your ways." That's okay with me, but I would rather have people learn their own way, and equally important is how they use what they learn. —Bear Heart

In chapter 2, we talked about some of the weaknesses and problems of baby boomers. In this chapter, we'll be looking primarily at the following generation, commonly known as generation X. The focus of these two chapters is admittedly negative, but it will definitely be balanced with positives as we progress through later chapters. Once again, we'll be addressing the issues of children in particular. When you begin planning and implementing changes to take back your neighborhoods, familiarity with the strengths, weaknesses, fears, and concerns of those with whom you will be working will be a tremendous asset. Once you know what to watch for, you will be much more successful in developing a neighborhood campus that works for your entire community.

Poverty and Welfare

"Poverty is the worst form of violence," Mahatma Gandhi said. George Bernard Shaw wrote much the same in the preface of *Major Barbara:* "The greatest of evils and the worst of crimes is poverty." If, as some have suggested, we can define evil as something that sucks the life, the aliveness, out of what it touches, then poverty is indeed an evil, violent crime. Poverty assaults the spirit, undermines virtue, and thrives on desperation. With no second thoughts, poverty destroys the hope of those neighborhoods in which it thrives.

There are two ways to define poverty. Absolute deprivation is "the inability to afford minimal standards of food, clothing, shelter, and healthcare." The other definition, which is what we'll be using primarily, is relative deprivation. Relative deprivation is "the inability to maintain the standards customary in the society" (Robertson 1987, 276). Another way to describe relative deprivation is as the poverty level, represented by the income necessary to purchase what society defines as a minimally acceptable standard of living.

In 1993, an annual income of $14,763 marked the poverty level for a family of four. Just over 15 percent of the population, 39.3 million persons, lived below poverty level. Average incomes of households in 1994 ranged from $36,959 for all families to $17,443 for female householders with no husband present. Male householders with no wife present earned an average of $26,467. Married couples averaged $43,005 a year, $51,204 if the wife was in the paid labor force and $30,218 if she was not (Wright 1995, 246).

Those numbers represent averages. They do not tell us that more than 34 percent of all female-headed households are poor. This is in part because women generally earn less than men, but the primary reason is the sharp increase in the number of unmarried mothers. Many unwed mothers are still young women who frequently lack job skills and may have to stay home to take care of their children (Robertson 1987, 277).

One child of every five lives in poverty. In 1990, 3 million women who had never married were raising children under the age of twenty-one. Less than 15 percent of those women were receiving child support; in fact, less than a quarter of non-custodial fathers provide court-mandated child support (Aburdene 1992, 240; Moynihan 1986, 167). By the year 2000, the number of single-parent households will outnumber two-parent families by five times and half of our children will be poor (Moynihan 1986, 142).

In 1990, median weekly earnings for women working full time (74 percent of all working women) were $348. These figures represent an increase of 2.9 percent from a year earlier, but women were still earning only 70 percent of men's median weekly earnings of $458 (Wright 1995, 259).

There are more than 14 million people on welfare, called Aid to Families with Dependent Children (AFDC). AFDC payments in 1994 amounted to $22.8 million (Wright 1995, 131). "Welfare is a direct result of couples not marrying, of fathers failing to support their offspring. Thus 90 percent of adults on welfare are mothers with dependent children; 67 percent of all welfare recipients are children under eighteen." These statements may be based on the fact that 94 percent of married couples are not poor, and that when couples marry they overwhelmingly tend to escape poverty (Naisbitt 1990, 170 and 46). In a speech he delivered July 22, 1996, in Denver, Colorado, President Clinton said, "If every person in this country paid the child support they're legally obligated to pay, and that they can pay, we could move 800,000 women and children off the welfare rolls today," as reported in the *Denver Post*, July 23, 1996. Fred Brown, *Denver Post* political editor, also reported that the president said, "It's 'a moral outrage and a social disaster' when parents won't support their children. . . . It's wrong to expect taxpayers to pick up the costs of parents who desert their children. 'It is a cold, inadequate substitute for having a parent do the right thing.'"

The US has no explicit family policy or family support system other than AFDC and modest tax preferences for families with dependent children. We are the only country whose main cash benefit is primarily for single mothers, and they lose the benefit and their health insurance if they work full time. Benefits in this country are usually available to only the poorest of families. What's more, they don't prevent poverty; they only help some people already living in it (Hopfensperger 1996).

We've sort of worked ourselves into a corner with regard to welfare. As a nation, our pioneer values work together with our fear of anything flavored by socialism; they work against reforms that would guarantee minimal benefits and security for all children, regardless of financial status. Later we'll talk more about the European system of benefits, which despite its negatives has many positives that make it worthy of consideration. Welfare is an issue that will continue to be fought politically—we certainly can't resolve it here—but the pros and cons are important considerations for many neighborhoods.

Crime

Headlines, studies, comments about statistics, and even everyday conversations all reflect that people are worried about crime in their communities. This is not surprising, considering that in 1990 almost twenty-four of every 1,000 households were touched by crime. Bob Dole (1996), former senator and 1996 presidential candidate, wrote in a recent article: "As we head into the 21st century, one of the greatest threats facing our country is not a foreign enemy, but the epidemic of violence that has already destroyed so many of our communities and now threatens every segment of our society. America's crime rate is the highest of any industrialized democracy. In 1994, Americans experienced more than 42 million crimes, including 11 million violent crimes. The annual cost of violent crimes is over $400 billion." He went on to say, "What is both heartbreaking and terrifying is that our young people constitute the fastest-growing category of criminals."

Indeed, 1993 figures reflect that law enforcement agencies made approximately 11.8 million arrests for all criminal infractions except traffic violations. The greatest numbers of arrests were for driving under the influence of drugs or alcohol (1.2 million), larceny or theft (1.3 million), simple assault (1 million), and drug abuse (1 million). A total of 45 percent of the persons arrested were under the age of twenty-five, 17 percent were under eighteen, and 6 percent were under fifteen. This under-twenty-five age group was responsible for 47 percent of all violent crime arrests and 58 percent of all property crime arrests. And contrary to what the movies and television depict, most of those arrested (67 percent) were white.

According to victimization rates (rates per 1,000 people age twelve or older), youngsters aren't only committing these crimes. In 1993, 246 out of every 1,000 victims of all crimes were between twelve and nineteen years old. Figures from 1990 indicate that 82 percent of homicides among teenagers aged fifteen to nineteen were associated with firearms. The victims of most kinds of crime are most likely to be black, young, poor, urban, and except for rape and domestic violence, male (Wright 1995, 281–84).

Juvenile delinquency is enormously damaging to the health and well-being of the nation's families and communities. To elaborate on some of Mr. Dole's figures, on a single day in 1985 public and private detention and correctional facilities held more than 83,000 children under the age of nineteen. We spend an average of more than $40,000 a year to care for an incarcerated juvenile. Vandalism in schools costs more than $200 million a year, and vandalism directed at personal property is even more expensive. Many costs are harder to measure—the effects of classroom disruption, the poor quality of life in high-crime neighborhoods, the juvenile offender's loss of education and earning potential, and the emotional and financial burdens borne by families of offenders and victims, to name a few.

Programs designed in the 1970s to follow a policy of removing status offenders (truants, runaways, liquor law violators) from public youth facilities have been no more effective than imprisonment. The alternative approaches these programs used included counseling, social work, and restitution programs in which offenders were obliged to compensate their victims by fines or community service. These measures "can be described as secondary prevention—measures that take effect after a crime has been committed and usually after the child is referred to social services by a court of law. But at that point it is often too late; the child has already developed a pattern of antisocial behavior that is difficult to change" (Zigler 1994).

Disadvantaged children often become school dropouts, 45 to 50 percent in large metropolitan areas. Some of them join street gangs, deal drugs, and commit violent acts including murder. Members of street gangs represent less than 1 percent of our population, yet they terrorize inner districts of every big city in our country. The gangs recruit young males, ten to twelve years old, to be their runners or fetchers. When old enough to become members, these youngsters must pledge loyalty to their gang. They do so because they have finally found a group that satisfies their need to belong and in which they feel needed and worthy. Gang members find their identity in a society that fears them. Such immersion in crime often numbs gang members to any feelings of remorse or guilt (Auletta 1982, 29). These young people are not beyond redemption, but they constitute a significant part of the crime problem in our communities.

Jon D. Hull, in an August 2, 1993, issue of *Time*, said that in Omaha, Nebraska, people were shocked by drive-by shootings in their middle-class communities as well as in the poorer neighborhoods. Hull's article, entitled "A Boy and His Gun," reported that the residents had trouble believing that their teenage boys carried pistol-grip, sawed-off shotguns that were easy to hide and required no skill to aim.

One fourteen-year-old said the gun gave him "power, authority and respect." During a four-month period, he participated in "nine drive-by shootings, aiming mostly at cars and houses."

"I'm not actually aiming at anybody," the boy said. "But once my older brother missed a baby's head by a quarter of an inch. It was in all of the news."

In a poll taken at ninety-six schools across the nation, "15 percent of students in the sixth through the twelfth grades said they had carried a handgun within the past thirty days, 11 percent said they had been shot at, and 59 percent said they knew where to get a gun if they need it." At a community meeting, one of the parents stood to speak. "I've been to four funerals in North Omaha, all kids," he said. "Can't young people get together without slaughtering each other?" (Hull 1993).

Kenneth Clark, author of *Dark Ghetto*, wrote: "The dark ghetto is institutionalized pathology; it is chronic, self-perpetuating pathology; it is the futile attempt by those in power to confine that pathology so as to prevent the spread of its contagion to the 'larger community.' . . . It would follow that one would find in the ghetto such symptoms of social disorganization and disease as high rates of juvenile delinquency, venereal disease among young people, narcotic addiction, illegitimacy, homicide" (Moynihan 1986, 23–24).

Life in violent neighborhoods often traumatizes children, who may suffer from posttraumatic disorders. "If children have the right to a happy and safe childhood they also have the right to scream out their rage and fear and to be heard and supported when their safety and joy are breached" (Garbarino 1992, 201). One characteristic of our generation X young people is that they have learned to "be tough" and methodical (DeWitt 1995). They don't scream out their rage and fear. And since posttraumatic disorders often present some time after the triggering incident, it is often not easy to connect later problems with the source.

Victims of child abuse and domestic violence don't scream out their fear and rage, either. In 1991, there were 1,767,673 reports of child abuse involving 2,695,010 children, according to the Statistical Abstract of the United States, 1993. "Sociological research has revealed an astonishing amount of family violence—between spouses, between parents and off-spring, and among the offspring themselves." About a fifth of all murders in the US are committed by a relative of the victim, and in half the cases that relative is the spouse. Husbands and wives are equally likely to kill each other. Physical child abuse is more common than any of us would like to admit, and child sexual abuse is equally dismaying. Again, child abuse is usually perpetrated by a family member or, in many cases, members (Robertson 1987, 351).

While researching the subjects of child abuse and domestic violence, we found an interesting absence of statistical information in the usual sources. While that information is certainly readily available, the question, "Why are those figures not right there next to other violent crimes in the almanacs and sociology texts?" seemed worth considering. Several possibilities present themselves.

First, victims of violence and abuse often feel devalued. Victims may fear profoundly for their lives, and often rightly so. In the case of sexual abuse, the perpetrator may threaten or demand a promise of secrecy from the child. Victims often don't report incidents for these reasons, so statistics would only reflect reported crimes.

Second, the victims of abuse often don't realize that it is wrong and should be reported. If the abusive cycle has been perpetuated through several family generations, as it often is, the victim may simply not realize family life can be any other way. A child who has grown up in a family in which mom hits dad, dad really hits mom, brother slugs brother, uncle goes into sister's room at night, and so on, may just assume everyone's family is like that. What's worse, if the child is not exposed to people and families who do not behave that way, he or she will grow up thinking such behavior is okay.

Third, while domestic violence by definition is considered physical, abuse can be and often is mental or verbal. And the effects can be just as devastating as those from physical abuse. In some ways, mental abuse can be even more damaging, because it is so difficult for the victim to identify and to describe to other people.

And fourth, the domain of abuse contains the material for fabrication and unfounded accusations. There is not always physical evidence of abuse and false accusations are not always intentional. Unintentional false accusations have received some publicity in recent years, and usually those we hear about have to do with memories of childhood abuse recovered by adults. As part of a detailed, easy-to-read discussion of the memory and how it works, Michael D. Yapko, Ph.D. and clinical psychologist (1994, 70–71), wrote:

> Other factors have been identified that influence the accuracy of memory, including (1) the person's motivation to notice, interpret, and remember; (2) the expectations that lead one to "see only what one expects to see," and not what is really there; (3) the methods used to retrieve memory, which can suggest additions or deletions to a remembered experience that alter its face completely (a point especially relevant to the process of recovering repressed memories); (4) the relationship with an outside memory investigator, which may increase or decrease responsiveness to prompts; and (5) the person's personality and reactions to memory gaps that may exist (one person may accept them as gaps, while another may have a need to fill them in, ever with misinformation, as in a process called "confabulation").

When a person confabulates a memory, he or she may be absolutely positive that the event occurred and absolutely convincing when talking to others about it. The problem is, some of these confabulations probably end up in the statistics, no matter how carefully checked. For whatever reasons, we must read statistics about some crimes with a certain awareness of the possibilities for skewed data. For example, of those 2,695,010 children involved in reports of child abuse mentioned earlier, only 811,709 were substantiated. The qualifying note reads that there was sufficient evidence under state law to conclude that mistreatment occurred or that the child was at risk of mistreatment.

Substance Abuse and Mental Illness

Many of us think of mental illness as some devastating problem confined to only a few, readily identified deviates. This misconception is just not true. Darrel Reigh, M.D., is director of the division of epidemiology and services research at the National Institute of Mental Health (NIMH). In a recent article in *Family Circle* magazine, he said, "People hear the term mental illness and immediately think the worst. But mental illnesses are just like physical illnesses—they can be as mild as a cold or as serious as a life-threatening infection."

Substance abuse and mental illness are each important subjects on their own. They are also often difficult to separate. While we can't fully discuss the causes of substance abuse or all the symptoms of mental illness, we can highlight a few important points. One such point is that often an illness such as depression can initiate substance abuse; just as often the abuse can result in such an illness as depression. If we're going to talk about substance abuse, we should note that the single most common cause of relapse to drug abuse in the US today is untreated depression and anxiety (*The Counselor* 1996, March/April, 5).

The Harvard Mental Health Letter (October 1994) revealed that at least 11 million people (about 6 percent of the adult population) have an episode of depression each year, according to an Epidemiologic Catchment Area Survey. Total cost of the disorder has been estimated at $44 billion. Twenty-eight percent of that figure is the direct cost of medical, psychiatric, and drug treatment; 17 percent is the result of the more than 18,000 associated suicides (at least one half of all people who commit suicide are severely depressed); and 55 percent, or $24 billion, is the effect of absenteeism and lowered productivity among the 72 percent of depressed persons who are in the labor force. The cost of absenteeism and lost productivity is about $180 per year per employee, or $3000 per year per depressed employee.

Research sponsored by NIMH reveals that nearly 16 percent of the US population suffers from a major mental illness or substance abuse in any one month. The most pervasive of these illnesses are depression (5.2 percent), phobia (6.3 percent), obsessive-compulsive disorder (1.3 percent), alcohol addiction (2.8 percent), and drug addiction (1.3 percent). Twenty percent of families are affected by severe mental illness in their lifetime. Mental illnesses are a leading cause of all hospital admissions, accounting for patients in 21 percent of hospital beds (*Mental Illness* 1996).

One area of concern that doesn't necessarily qualify as substance abuse or mental illness, although it is often related to one or both, is suicide. In 1993, 31,230 people killed themselves, which is about one person every twenty minutes. An estimated 400,000 additional unsuccessful attempts were made. These figures are probably not reflective of actual suicides; many experts believe numerous suicides are categorized as accidents. More women than men attempt suicide, but fewer complete their attempts. In 1993, 6,250 women committed suicide, as compared to 24,990 men that same year.

The suicide rate for youths aged fifteen to twenty-four has tripled since 1950. In 1993, the number that committed suicide was 4960; 310 children between five and fourteen years of age did so as well (Wright 1995, 220).

The factors that put people at risk for suicide are numerous. About 70 percent of those who attempt suicide have been diagnosed as depressed. However, many depressed people never attempt suicide, and not all who do commit suicide are depressed. Those who abuse substances are at highest risk for suicide. Drugs and alcohol lower a person's control significantly, so he or she may act on a suicidal impulse. Use of drugs and alcohol indicates low impulse control in general and a low tolerance for frustration and stress. Finally, the alcohol and drugs themselves provide the means by which to end life.

For suicides in general, the high-risk profile would be someone who has previously attempted suicide; has directly or indirectly threatened suicide; is chronically ill or isolated (senior citizens may fall into this category); is experiencing bereavement; is suffering financial distress; is having domestic problems; is severely depressed or psychotic; has a family history of suicide; and uses alcohol, barbiturates, or hallucinogenic drugs.

To those factors, we can add some characteristics of the high-risk adolescent. The suicidal adolescent's profile would include age (fifteen to twenty-four); sex (twice as many boys commit suicide as girls, although girls attempt suicide more often); intelligence (gifted adolescents are more prone to attempt suicide); advanced physical development; being unduly self-critical or perfectionistic, and feelings of helplessness and vulnerability. Family background is very important, too, especially if the child is in an environment of family violence or intense marital discord, or has experienced the loss of a parent. (Hafen 1986, 26–42).

Some other facts you may not know or might have forgotten, from *The Counselor*, November/December 1995 and March/April 1996:

• A national survey conducted for Drug Strategies and cited by the Center for Substance Abuse Research found that 43 percent of Americans have changed the way they live because of drug-related problems. Types of changes include "when or where you shop" and "taking security precautions in your home." The telephone survey was conducted in February 1995.

• A significant number of ten- to thirteen-year-olds revealed that they expect they may fall into the traps of teenage pregnancy, and drug and alcohol use. A study, sponsored by KidsPeace: the National Center for Kids in Crisis reported that nearly half of the more than 1,000 children surveyed—47 percent—reported bleak expectations. When asked about their future, children as young as ten said they thought they might well be unhappy in their lives. More than half of the children (54 percent) said they are concerned that they might contract AIDS. At the same time, 41 percent said they are concerned they might get involved in using drugs, and 44 percent said they believe they might start using alcohol.

• The Centers for Disease Control and Prevention (CDC) report that over one-third of the 80,691 new AIDS cases reported in 1994 were associated with injection drug use (IDU). According to the Center for Substance Abuse Research, most IDU-related AIDS cases were among heterosexuals, making injection drug use the most prevalent mode of transmission among heterosexuals.

• According to an August 21, 1995, report from the Center for Substance Abuse Research, 69 percent of 2,801 householders surveyed believe that drug abuse is a fairly serious or very serious problem among young adults (aged seventeen to twenty-one) in their community, while 62 percent believe this is true of alcohol abuse. Survey respondents also cited dysfunctional families, lack of job skills, and teenage pregnancy as serious problems facing young people.

• Recently released data from the 1995 Monitoring the Future Study show that marijuana use continues to increase among eighth, tenth and twelfth graders.

• As many as 40 percent of all hospital admissions are related to the misuse of alcohol or drugs.

• Nearly three out of every ten homicide victims in New York City in the early 1990s had evidence of cocaine in their bodies when they died, according to research funded by the National Institute of Drug Abuse. "Homicide victims may have provoked violence through irritability, paranoid thinking or verbal or physical aggression, which are known to be pharmacological effects of cocaine," the researchers suggest.

As we mentioned in chapter 2, it's not just these young men and women themselves who are affected by problems associated with substance abuse or mental illness. Consider the unborn and newborn babies of these children who have not had the benefit of adequate sex and health education.

Nancy Gibbs (1993) told us that the federal government spends over $5 million a year on infants born with drug addiction. According to the National Association for Perinatal Addiction Research and Education (NAPARE), about one newborn out of every ten was exposed to drugs while in the womb. In large cities, the number is more than 20 percent.

Fetal alcohol syndrome is still the leading cause of mental retardation, but the number of women using other drugs has been on the rise for years. More than 1 million pregnant women use cocaine, as do about 7 percent of teens in the twelfth grade. Crack, a cheap type of cocaine, has made the situation worse since it is so easy to ingest by smoking. Since the 1980s, many of these women have used other drugs as well, so many crack babies literally absorb a brew of drugs while in the womb.

The effects such drugs have on developing fetuses are severe; most crack babies have deficiencies of one sort or another, including physical and mental disabilities, as well as severe emotional difficulties. And these effects have a price. In California, it has been found that care for newborn crack babies is thirteen times as expensive as for normal newborns. Since the birth mothers place many of these babies in foster homes, that cost will continue to increase. New York City will spend $365 million over the next ten years on special education. Boston will spend $13,000 a year on special education for each child compared to $5,000 a year for a normal child.

After birth, these babies often continue to suffer poverty, neglect, and violence. Although more crack babies are born to women who are poor and in minority groups, many are born to upper- and middle-class mothers. These births are just hidden better from the public.

Those children born in the mid-1980s, are now entering our schools, adding an overwhelming burden to a system already encumbered with a multitude of problems. Crack kids required specially trained teachers and programs.

Dr. Ira Chasnoff at the Chicago-based NAPARE studied three hundred babies prenatally exposed to drugs. They, along with their mothers, received intensive postnatal intervention. Of ninety children tested at age three, 90 percent showed normal intelligence, 70 percent had no behavioral problems, and 60 percent did not need speech therapy (Gibbs 1993, 60–65).

The Harvard Mental Health Letter (September 1995) detailed further information on that study. The study grouped the mothers according to their drug usage during pregnancy: thirty-three used cocaine, usually along with other drugs; twenty-four used marijuana, alcohol, and opiates in various combinations, but not cocaine; twenty-five used no drugs, except tobacco in some cases. The last group served as the control group.

The differences between the children at three years were fairly minimal, as Gibbs observed. However, children in both drug groups were less attentive while performing difficult tasks. Their parents reported more destructive behavior, and more aggression in the case of the cocaine group. Children in the cocaine group also scored lower on verbal reasoning than the control children, but only if they were living with a parent who continued to use drugs. Children exposed to marijuana scored lower in abstract visual reasoning. The authors warned against premature conclusions about the ill effects of prenatal drug exposure, considering the many other possible causes of the children's problems.

So, as with most issues, the effects of prenatal drugs on children are debatable from both sides. Knowing what we all know about the negative effects of drugs on older children and adults, there seems to be no plausible argument for taking drugs during pregnancy unless under close medical supervision. The problem isn't just the drugs, though.

Surprisingly often, a mother of young children is hampered or even incapacitated by depression. Women of child-bearing age develop clinical depression at twice the rate of men the same age. Those episodes can last as long as three years. About half of depressed mothers who recover have a recurrence of depression within two years. As a result, many children spend their formative years in the care of a woman who is depressed. Characteristic symptoms of depression can include sadness, hopelessness, indecisiveness, thoughts of suicide, insomnia, fatigue, inability to concentrate, and general loss of interest in life. Clearly these symptoms are not conducive to effective parenting.

Depressed mothers may fail to supervise their children adequately. They also convey their unhappiness to the child. They tend to be irritable, silent, and insufficiently playful. Often they reduce the child's self-esteem, social contacts, and popularity with peers by neglecting the home, dress, and grooming.

If a depressed mother is also experiencing marital problems—and most do—the combination can be devastating for the kids. The attendant crises such as job and financial losses and conflict with family and neighbors create stress for all concerned. Depressed people tend to drive others away, so they can feel they receive insufficient support from family and friends. Feeling emotionally neglected themselves, depressed mothers may fail to provide their children with enough needed attention and support. If this depression is combined with mood swings and other characteristic symptoms of drug use, the life script a very young child puts together can become very warped.

As a result of less-satisfying interactions with their mother, babies of depressed moms may show signs of depression themselves. Sadness, submissive helplessness, and social withdrawal are common, and often the baby does not achieve the crucial security and emotional attachment he or she needs.

Older children of depressed parents are three to four times more likely to have adjustment problems. They may demonstrate aggressive and disruptive behavior, attention deficits, and other disorders, as well as depression, anxiety, and phobias (How Much . . . 1994).

＝＋＋＝

If any plan to take back our neighborhoods is to be successful, generation X will be important to its execution. We've mentioned a few characteristics of this generation as a group. Additional characteristics follow, with a caution that as with all generalizations, there will be exceptions. These are guidelines only, and suggested with the intention that they offer some insight in creating and fulfilling your plan.

Generation Xers range in age from thirteen to thirty; 48 million of them were born between 1965 and 1982. These young people, based on statistical evidence, are different from older generations. Drinking, drugs, violence, suicide, and emotional problems are more common in generation X than any other previous group. By age sixteen, they have seen 18,000 murders on television, more than 350,000 commercials and hundreds of hours of news programs. They pride themselves on not being taken in by the news media, and feel disdain for marketing ploys. They tend to have sex earlier but marry later, and more of them have unplanned pregnancies. Generation X is the first generation of latchkey kids grown up, and 40 percent of them have been victims of parental divorce.

These young people seem to be looking for one right answer—the quick fix. If they ask a question, they want an answer. If you tell them they need to figure out the answer for themselves, that message often translates in their minds to the assumption you do not have an answer.

Just as many baby boomers were the first generation raised on television, generation Xers are the first group of young people raised on computers. As a result, they are more comfortable in the black-and-white, pragmatic world of logical thinking. In contrast, when inundated with choices, options, and possibilities, generation Xers often become caught up in a myriad of details that render them incapable of making timely decisions.

Many generation Xers grew up in families touched by divorce, and many of those with "traditional" families saw little of their parents, as both worked full time. Many of them are used to being let down by parents who are too busy with work. They can be overwhelmed by the "big picture," working better with short-term goals and objectives that allow them to work on one issue at a time. If they establish their own goals, they will stay on task better.

Generation Xers like to keep their options open. Too many rules, expectations, and time demands are not their cup of tea. They may not share the work ethic or sense of commitment of their elder counterparts. They did, after all, grow up in families where divorce or workaholic parents or both were commonplace. So they learned that commitments can be broken and that working all the time can alienate a person from family and friends (DeWitt 1995).

Now, armed with all this knowledge that is really only a drop in the bucket, we boomers and Xers can go out there and try to learn our own ways to reclaim our neighborhoods.

Kimi Gray,
the Miracle Worker,
and Christmas in April

*No surer expression of superiority is than to treat people primarily as victims. . . .
Victimism is a disease that blights our best-intended social programs . . . because
it attacks the ability and inclination of people to look after themselves. . . . We
teach drug addicts they are essentially victims of society . . . and since society
isn't going to change . . . we also teach the drug addict that he is essentially
hopeless.* —William Raspberry, Syndicated Columnist, Washington Post

*If schools weren't compulsory, if schools were autonomous and were run by the
people in them, then we could learn without being subdued and stupefied in the
process. And, perhaps, we could regain control of our society.*
—Jerry Farber, The Student as Nigger

The Kenilworth-Parkside Resident Management Corporation
in Washington D.C., is a prime example of changing a neighborhood from the inside out. The residents of one Washington
area successfully took back responsibility for and management
of their own neighborhood. Their story is a demonstration of
shared responsibility and how it relates to the stability of the
family and the neighborhood.

Taking Back Our Neighborhoods

In an article within the "American Ideas" section in *Time* magazine, December 12, 1988, Jerome Cramer described the concept of shared responsibility and how it affected the families of one neighborhood. The hero of the story was Kimi Gray, a welfare mother of five children and an authentic miracle worker.

Kimi Gray lived in a wretched housing project with 3,500 residents. Broken toilets and limited heating were typical of the living conditions in this project. Kimi despaired that all her neighbors had given up hope for anything better. They were broken families living on streets of broken dreams in a neighborhood decayed beyond repair. Frustrated by the project's poor management, she believed the tenants themselves could do a better job of managing their own neighborhood.

In 1972, Kimi Gray began a campaign to achieve exactly that. She went to the city and asked that the tenants be charged with management of the project. The authorities ignored her, so she organized the residents to register to vote.

Armed with the signatures of 12,000 tenants of public housing, all now registered voters, Kimi petitioned the mayor to turn over management of the project to the residents. Finally, the district granted the tenants permission to set up their own management. In 1982, Kimi Gray became the chairperson of Kenilworth-Parkside Resident Management Corporation.

Without any training in physical plant management, the residents now faced actually managing a run-down project. "It was a crisis that brought us together," said Kimi Gray. "We want[ed] to bring families back together, [to] restore our pride and respect."

Eventually, the residents were able to buy shares in their units. Businesses created by the management corporation included a daycare center, a barber shop, a beauty shop, a moving company, and a construction company. The corporation created employment for over one hundred residents.

The organization developed strict rules for sharing responsibility for the maintenance of the grounds, buildings, and individual homes. Repairing broken plumbing was just one example of this shared responsibility. The rules required that each family have one member take six weeks of training in such subjects as personal budget, pest control, and basic home repairs. Residents were fined when they broke the rules. Those who used the daycare center had to be working or looking for a job. If families repeatedly refused to conform to the rules, the penalty was eviction. At the time the article was written, only five families had been removed in five years.

After six years, the Kenilworth-Parkside Resident Management Corporation had reduced the number of residents on welfare from 85 percent to 2 percent. Teenage pregnancies decreased from 70 percent to 12 percent. Administrative costs for the project dropped two-thirds. Implementation of this tenant management saved the district and the federal government $5.7 million in operating expenses.

According to Robert Woodson, head of the National Center for Neighborhood Enterprise, "The federal and state governments have spent nearly $1 trillion over the past twenty years in a largely failed effort to fight poverty. Now Kimi and the others are taking it out of the hands of the professionals and giving jobs to tenants. . . . Kimi and other leaders are the last, best hope for many of these public-housing projects. Tenant managers can't offer guarantees, but they hold great promise. The only thing worse than poverty is accepting the status quo."

Kimi Gray brought more than hope to people once considered unemployable and too dependent on the system to ever change. She forged a path that allowed them to reclaim their self-esteem, pride, and dignity. She helped strengthen the nuclear family. Residents worked together, sharing responsibility for their neighborhood and their futures.

"Being poor doesn't give you the right to be dirty or lazy," said Kimi Gray. She serves as an inspiration to all those who are not satisfied with life the way it is today. Poverty can be disarmed if the poor share responsibility for training their children, managing their neighborhoods, and building hope for the future.

One person can make a difference; one person can bring about change for the common good. Kimi Gray proved it.

⋙ ⋘

Another example of change in action, this time from the outside in and on the other side of the country, is the work done by an organization named Christmas in April. Judy Johnstone shared the story of this group in the July 1996 edition of *Crosswinds*, a newspaper published in Albuquerque and distributed throughout New Mexico.

Christmas in April is a national organization dedicated to rehabilitating houses for homeowners who are no longer able to maintain their properties because of low income, disability, or age. Once, after the organization renovated a house in Midland, Texas, the delighted homeowner exclaimed, "Why, it's just like having Christmas in April!" The name stuck. However, since the April weather in Santa Fe is often snowy and blustery, Christmas in April does its annual one-day blitz on housing in June. The 1996 blitz took place on June 8. That day, two hundred volunteers for the Santa Fe chapter rehabilitated ten homes, dozens of local businesses and banks, and a couple of churches.

One of the homes belonged to Francisco. The seventy-something Dallas Cowboys fan and lover of flowers shares a mobile home with his sister. Years ago, Francisco was so badly injured that only after two operations and painstaking effort was he able to learn to walk and talk again. After neighbors in their group housing complained about Francisco's wheelchair, he and his sister moved into the mobile home with the tiny surrounding yard.

When Christmas in April showed up, ready to paint and repair doors and windows, they added a special touch: flowers and bricks to line a new flowerbed and pave an area in front of the storage shed. "Francisco loved the flowers, but declined to have his bedroom repainted. He likes the Cowboy blue that serves as a background for his memorabilia of the team."

Another Santa Fe resident, Aurelia, shares the home her husband Pantaleon built in 1943 with her granddaughter and three great-grandchildren. The eighty-eight-year-old has no one to help maintain the house since her father died and her brother moved into a nursing home.

When a volunteer contractor, several skilled tradesmen, and some amateur painters came to the home in what is now the historic district, they completed the repairs Aurelia could not. The transformation was noticeable. Quite a bit of paint, combined with eight new windows, three exterior doors, a roof patch, and a new kitchen counter, worked miracles.

Daughter Rosina said, "Mother's house will be warmer this winter, and we expect the utility bills to be much lower."

Christmas in April USA is based in Washington, D.C. The organization has about 180 affiliate groups in fifty states. Interestingly enough, it was founded by "an oil scout named Bobby Trimble, who thought the idea of a barn raising should be applied to cities and towns," *Crosswinds* reports.

4
The Neighborhood Campus:
An Overview

You are never given a wish without also being given the power to make it true.
You may have to work for it, however.
—Richard Bach, Illusions

So what's your neighborhood going to be like when you get through with it? You probably have some idea that it can be better, some vague picture in your mind of how it would look. Is your family happy there? Are they and your neighbors safe? Do you know something about who those people are, really are, besides just their names?

Perhaps even just knowing your neighbors' names is a big stretch for your imagination right now. Take a few minutes to think about how you'd like your community to be. You're only creating the picture in your mind, so be extravagant. You haven't told anybody yet, so for now it's just you visiting your dream world.

The next step is creating a vision. Vision is a fancy word all the books use to talk about an imaginary picture, but it's a good, short word that implies a picture with something more. Great things usually begin as a dream; a vision includes the promise that the dream can come true. In *Teaching the Elephant to*

Dance, James Belasco (1990, 98) said, "Vision is the difference between short-term 'hits' . . . and long-term change. Vision translates paper strategies into a way of life. Vision empowers people to change."

This chapter is an overview of the neighborhood campus and how you can put it together. The information provided should enable you to begin refining your vision and imagining how your neighborhood campus can be. There are a few critical points to remember about how to take a dream and begin forming it into a vision.

Detail is one very important characteristic of a vision you intend to make reality. Imagine your children playing safely outside, but then go back into the picture and add the details. Put some flowers in the yard across the street, a new coat of paint on the house next door. Oh, there are some of your neighbors chatting down the block while they watch the kids play. The more detail in your vision, the more powerful it becomes.

The other important point we'll introduce now is that you must begin to think of the vision as reality. This feat may require some changes in your perspective. If you look out your window, you can no longer just see bare dirt, cracked concrete, or run-down houses if that's your view. What you must see is the dream neighborhood in transition. Start looking for the raw material out there that will be the substance of your new creation.

Here's a brief example of the vision-to-reality process. The first page of the 1993 Downtown Aurora Visual Arts (DAVA) Annual Report contains their mission statement: "Recognizing that visual assets enhance the quality of life and building understanding between various elements of a community, Downtown Aurora Visual Arts will encourage, stimulate and coordinate a broad base of visual arts activities in the community with a specific emphasis on the value of our cultural heritage." In this statement, the founders of DAVA clarified their vision so they could communicate it to others.

DAVA was started with the intention of drawing from the strengths of a community located in an aging, downtown area but had grown into a Denver, Colorado, suburb. Like many communities, the suburban areas grew out and away from the old area known as Original Aurora. DAVA planned to become a part of the effort to rejuvenate Original Aurora by developing the arts as a positive social force in the community. Funded by a combination of grants and donations, DAVA worked with the Aurora Rehabilitation Authority, the Downtown Aurora Business Association, the Aurora Arts and Humanities Council, and elementary schools, as well as other groups and individuals.

One of DAVA's projects was to create a three-part clay program for schools that included education about background material, field trips, creation of clay art projects by students at the schools involved, and an exhibition of the children's work. Their 1994 goals included creation of a clay-tile mural on a brick wall of an old storefront building. The wall adjoined a small open area that had been rejuvenated with stone benches, trees, and large concrete planters for flowers.

The staff, which at the time of the annual report consisted of the director and one artist, combined their talents to teach groups of children artistic and ceramic skills. The goals and objectives DAVA set forth as part of the clay project are important, and are clearly defined in the report.

> In addition to the skills and concepts involved in the production of art objects, the goals and objectives of the Clay Project are to help these children, youth and families:
> - explore concepts of self
> - enhance verbal and nonverbal communication skills
> - participate in positive group interactions and collaborations
> - have contact with local, successful minority artists who serve as role models
> - reduce violent interactions within families and peer groups
> - develop cultural identity

The group developed a curriculum and a schedule, planned fund-raising efforts and drafted grant applications, and anticipated adding teaching assistants and interns. They planned to offer scholarships to children from low- to moderate-income families.

Local artists helped plan the overall design of the clay mural. The children participating made their own clay tiles with their own designs, painted and glazed them, and watched intently as they were fired in and brought from the kiln. Participants in the program and volunteers placed each shiny, unique tile into the mural design. During that year, a fascinating, brilliantly colored giant mosaic gradually transformed a boring old wall into a magnificent work of art. One can sit on one of the stone benches and enjoy the mural, just beyond the abundance of summer flowers in the planters. A casual stroll for a close-up look reveals the delightful individual tiles—faces of children, exotic creatures, representations of friendship and fellowship.

The transformed wall was part of the reality that came from DAVA's vision, defined in their mission statement. The process affected all those involved according to the goals and objectives they outlined, which were further clarification of the vision. Even people not involved were and continue to be affected by the mosaic. It's beautiful to look at, and knowledge about its creation is inspiring. Seeing the mural inevitably alters one's perception of "running into a brick wall."

To be consistent with the practice of thinking of a vision as reality in progress, we will talk about the neighborhood campus throughout this chapter as though it already exists. Your vision may differ from the outline here and from every other neighborhood campus, for that matter, but if the thought is there, the campus is there.

The Daycare Center

The daycare center's design addresses a number of the problems discussed in chapter 2. Children need a safe place with a high-quality program, well-trained staff, and individual attention. Parents need to know their children are well cared for in a healthy environment.

Staffed by well-paid, certified teachers working in conjunction with the parent training center, the daycare center also shares the benefits of a twenty-four-hour security guard program. Besides having role models available, in the form of teachers, parents, and other participants, children have the opportunity to be around uniformed security staff who offer a positive example of people in uniform.

A daycare center requires space, so the kindergarten room in the school is adapted to the needs of the center. Kindergarten was designed to provide children with the opportunity to socialize with other children as preparation for the first grade and their entry into compulsory education. The daycare center simply expands the benefits of a kindergarten program to include younger children.

The daycare center also offers seniors and older students in the neighborhood a chance to participate in the children's care. Private licensed daycare centers are unaffected and continue as they are, although some may be absorbed eventually by the neighborhood campus.

The Parent Training Center

At the parent training center, parents have access to information about subjects as diverse as how to nurture their children, manage a household, and develop a set of values and goals. Prenatal and postnatal care, parent effectiveness training, and communication skills are examples of courses and workshops offered through the center.

If you want to expand the parent training center program to include other subjects of interest and value to adults in general, you can draw singles and childless couples into participating at the campus. People who are experts in particular aspects of business and vocational training, crafters and artists, professionals of all types are often willing to offer seminars or workshops about their specialty for minimal or no fees. These people may be residents of your neighborhood, or they may live elsewhere but be equally committed to improving communities and the lot of all people. More and more often, it seems, we hear people say, "I've been fortunate, and I just want to give something back." Many people just enjoy sharing their passion, and would be delighted to work with your campus program.

The After-School Arts and Recreation Center

The after-school arts and recreation center is open to all students, seniors, and singles. This center is a joint effort between the school district and the parks and recreation department in your city. Certified classroom teachers are available to teach basic subjects—perhaps including remedial classes, English as a second language, and so on—from eight or nine o'clock in the morning. Arts and recreation are scheduled from two to six in the afternoon, assuring that the children are supervised in a secure place throughout the day.

The staff from the parks and recreation department work together with the certified teachers in the arts and physical education. Private professional teachers of ballet, modern dance, drama, photography, astronomy, and any number of other subjects participate as well.

Certified teachers and the staff of other social and civic agencies sharing responsibility in this manner is a new idea. Most large school districts around the country are trying to find ways to improve relations between the people in their communities, schools, and local governments. Arlington, Virginia, has twenty-two elementary schools that have after-school programs for children for which the parents pay two-thirds of the extra cost. Denver rents empty classrooms to nonprofit daycare associations. In New York City, two-thirds of the private schools provide full-day supervision.

Our public schools could use their buildings and grounds more effectively. Operation of a facility eight hours a day, one hundred eighty days a year, doesn't maximize a school's financial potential. In Highwood, Illinois, the Parks and Recreation Department cooperates with the school district, using empty classrooms and grounds at the end of the school day. The city pays the school district for use of its property, which in turn helps the school district balance its budget. Wilton, Connecticut has a similar plan (Packard 1983, 131–50).

The Health Center

"Childhood Diseases on the Rise," an article from *The Washington Post* reprinted in the *Seattle Times,* January 3, 1988, alerted readers that contagious diseases such as polio and measles are on the rise again. Once nearly eliminated, these illnesses may now be increasing in part because parents are uninformed, or cannot afford the costs of shots, or lack transportation to medical clinics. The health center keeps records of every child in the neighborhood beginning with prenatal development. The center provides for vaccinations and shots to be given at the proper times. New mothers have access to prenatal and postnatal care. Seniors can come in for checkups monthly.

If a parent becomes too ill to care for him- or herself and the rest of the family, outside help may be needed. In Germany, "grandmothers" are available twenty-four hours a day to go into a home and manage it until the parent is well again. There, the government pays for this service (Packard 1983, 353). Parents of sick children in Tucson, Arizona, can call a dispatcher twenty-four hours a day to ask for a daycare aide to come to their home. The aide stays with the children while the parents work (Gordon 1989). These support systems encourage family stability as well as workforce productivity.

A separate place is available in the daycare center for children with minor illnesses such as colds. In recent years, more daycare centers have offered "sniffles" programs for children with mild illnesses such as earaches, colds, and the flu when they are not in contagious stages. A full-time registered nurse is in charge. These programs not only boost the morale and productivity of working parents, they greatly decrease absenteeism (US Depart. of Labor 1983).

The Senior Center

Fewer than 5 percent of our children see their grandparents on a regular basis. Many grandparents now live far away from their children and grandchildren. Often left alone in older neighborhoods or living in retirement communities, they have little contact with their grandchildren, or any other children, for that matter.

No senior has to feel alone or lonely with the neighborhood campus in place. They can share up to three hot meals a day with the children at the campus. The neighborhood campus eliminates the need for older folks to travel across town—often a difficult and inconvenient prospect—to visit senior centers. They meet elderly neighbors, socialize, and participate in the after-school arts and recreation activities in their own neighborhood.

Elderly people, like all of us, have many of the same needs as children. They need to belong and to feel useful. The neighborhood campus gives seniors more opportunities to mix with younger people and children, expanding their opportunities to stay active and sharp.

The Twenty-Four-Hour Crisis Center

Abused adults and children often continue to suffer mistreatment because they have no place to go, or because they are afraid to leave. They may have no funds or family nearby, and they may be without hope for a better life. The neighborhood campus provides these people the prospect of immediate relief from their distress.

These abused adults and children are familiar with their neighborhood campus. They know the security guards and the workers in the twenty-four-hour crisis center. They know they can go to the campus and find protection. Within an hour, staff and volunteers can find a shelter for the victims and escort them there in safety.

Too many teenagers run away from home only to end up on the streets where they are further victimized. The crisis center offers a safe place in their own neighborhood where they can find help.

⟫⟪

A project serves as a common theme tying all the different components of the neighborhood center together. The project theme winds throughout the daycare, parent, and senior center programs. For this book, we used a curriculum based on ecology as an example. If ecology is the science of the relationship between living organisms and their environments, we could say that human ecology is the relationship between humans and their human environment.

The possibilities for an ecology curriculum, as well as the possibilities for other types of projects, are countless. For example, an effort to repair and rebuild neighborhood homes similar to the Christmas in April program described in the last chapter could be another great project. In fact, you might want to keep a pad and pencil nearby to list ideas for programs, workshops, and projects as they come to you. Appendix B contains a sample ecology-based curriculum for you to modify for your neighborhood campus, or to use as a model to create a different kind of curriculum for your project.

The elementary school is the most logical place to bring families in the neighborhood together to share in the benefits of a neighborhood campus. Elementary schools have been divided into districts in urban areas since the early 1900s. In many cases, the area served by an elementary school basically corresponds to the area you might define as a neighborhood.

The advantage of the neighborhood campus is that there are no changes made in any governmental agency or school administration. The only difference is in the distribution of the professional workers. Rather than working in centrally located offices and medical clinics, workers are assigned to the neighborhoods at the elementary schools or other locations of campuses. Their salaries and funding for the centers still come from the agencies they represent.

This overview presents only part of the foundation for taking back your neighborhood by creating a neighborhood campus. The next two chapters will help you reinforce this foundation by identifying and clarifying values and practicing the concept of shared responsibility.

5
Rebuilding a Set of Values

⚏

The village can no longer be defined as a place on a map, or a list of people or organizations, but its essence remains the same: it is the network of values and relationships that support and affect our lives. —Hillary Rodham Clinton

Years ago an individual talked about "my family, my neighborhood, my neighbors, my school, my church, my home," because these different groups were of value to the person. They defined who a person was and his or her place in the community. These days, "my family" may be scattered all over the country, if not the world. "My neighborhood" may be someplace to avoid, or simply a place to go away from. "My neighbors" are people often only seen, but not heard and not known. "My school" might be dangerous at worst, neutral at best, or different every year for those who move frequently. "My church" doesn't even exist for a number of people. "My home" for many is also a dangerous place, a place of conflict, or a place too seldom seen much less enjoyed.

Writing about values is a more difficult task than one might expect. What are values anyway? Sociologists say values are things we value. Okay, we value success, let's say. What is success? Your coworker's definition may be quite different from your own. You may value success as reaching a high-level corporate position and an income of six or more digits. Your friend may value success as doing what she loves, never mind the income. Another person may define success as raising healthy, well-adjusted children. Yet another may consider staying alive another day a huge success. Can we say, then, that success is a value we share, but define as individuals?

What makes values important? If each of us lived alone, never seeing another person, the question would be merely a mental exercise. But we don't live apart from other people, and values are, well, valuable when we have to deal with others. It's useful, for instance, if the people we are around share a value for life. We can then rest assured that we can go about our business without fear of losing our lives at the hand of another person, at least not purposely. The problem is that some of us value life, but many others don't. How do we know that? Check out the crime section in chapter 3 again.

Values are also important because they help us make decisions. French philosopher Jean-Paul Sartre said, "We create ourselves by virtue of our choices." When we know our values, we have power to control the direction of our lives by the choices we make. If, for example, you hold family as a value, then you can more readily turn down a job that requires a great deal of travel or time away from home. The conflict arises when another value causes you to waver. If you also hold achievement as a value and the job is a promotion, then you have to determine what is of the most value to you. The importance is that you have some ground to stand on as you decide which way to jump—into a job that probably doesn't have a promise of longevity, or back to your family relationships that, if nurtured, hold the potential for permanence. Your values give you *power*, because no one else can tell you what they are or what to do. You are not at the mercy of anyone or anything else.

When we don't provide children with the foundation of values, we deny them power. If we don't make certain that they have enough education and enough role models to enable them to wrestle with value definition and comparison, we throw them to the mercy of others—other children, other adults, the media. We can't make children adopt our values; we can teach them to choose their own values with awareness. If we behave consistently with our values, then our children can see that our values work (if indeed they do). A child raised to accept human dignity as a value, who has been encouraged to think about what dignity is and talk about different ways dignity shows up, will probably never be abused. But if abused because of circumstances beyond his or her control, that child will still retain the power to not allow another person's actions to affect that core of dignity and self-worth.

Let's reconsider some of those questions from the introduction. What values seem apparent in the current state of our neighborhood? Are the apparent values the values we want? We might assume our values are the right values and therefore are (and, we think, rightly should be) shared by others. This assumption does not recognize the reality of the present status of our environment. The statistics tell us clearly that our values are not shared by everyone else. Seeing the reality is noticing that a high crime rate reflects a significant number of people who do not value life, or property, or human dignity, for example. Unfortunately, we can't change that problem all at once. Fortunately, we can attack the problem with vigor and persistence and start the process of change as a legacy to the future.

Reestablishing values is work. It is a task that requires personal and group questioning of what's going on in the neighborhood and in society. One of the most important questions about a value is, Where does that come from—what is the source of this value we're talking about? Another good question is, Is this a value we've just continued to believe in because we haven't thought about it, or is it one that is still valid for us?

We can't tell you what values you and your neighbors should have. What we can tell you is that defining your values as a community begins the transformation of your neighborhood from just a place into a village. Sometimes you have to find those values by considering what actions society punishes. We know that as a society, we value freedom, partly because we punish people who kidnap other people and deny them their freedom.

Stephen Covey suggests that values come from principles. He wrote (1989, 24):

> Each of us has many, many maps in our head, which can be divided into two main categories: maps of *the way things are*, or *realities*, and maps of *the way things should be*, or *values*. We interpret everything we experience through these mental maps. We seldom question their accuracy; we're usually even unaware that we have them. We simply *assume* the way we see things is the way they really are or the way they should be.
>
> And our attitudes and behaviors grow out of those assumptions. The way we see things is the source of the way we think and the way we act.

Covey says we only think we're objective. We actually see the world not as it is, but as we are, as we are conditioned to see it. There are principles that govern human effectiveness. These principles are "natural laws that are woven into the fabric of every civilized society throughout history and comprise the roots of every family and institution that has endured and prospered. The degree to which our mental maps accurately describe the territory does not alter its existence" (1989, 28–34).

Let's look at a few lists for a minute. Covey's list of principles includes

- integrity and honesty;
- human dignity (as in the US Declaration of Independence, which states, "We hold these truths to be self-evident: that all men are created equal and endowed by their Creator with certain inalienable rights, that among these are life, liberty and the pursuit of happiness");

- service;
- quality or excellence;
- potential and growth;
- patience, nurturance, and encouragement.

Finally, before we move on from Stephen Covey, consider the question he posed (1991, 184): "How are we going to get work done?" In this particular instance, he was talking about work as in an organization. For our purposes, we can consider "work" to be the work of maximizing the potential of our children, ourselves, our families, our neighborhoods, and ultimately our society. We need to have some kind of agreement to formalize and organize our relationships so we can do this work. Covey calls it a "win-win performance agreement," in which the parties involved share a common vision based on common principles. With such a shared vision or agreement, everyone can do his or her part to accomplish the vision without constant monitoring.

Robertson (1987, 62–65) defines values as "socially shared ideas about what is good, right, and desirable. . . .Values are abstract, general concepts. . . ." He uses education as an example of the distinction between values and norms, which are "shared rules or guidelines that prescribe the behavior appropriate in a given situation." If a society values education highly, he explains, then its norms will make provision for mass schooling. American values, then, Robertson says, based on the research of Robin Williams (not *that* Robin Williams, but the one who wrote *American Society* in 1970), are the following:
- achievement and success,
- activity and work,
- moral orientation,
- humanitarianism,
- efficiency and practicality,
- progress,
- material comfort,
- equality,

- freedom,
- external conformity,
- science and rationality,
- nationalism-patriotism,
- democracy,
- individualism,
- group superiority.

Note how closely Covey's principles are related to Robertson's values; note also some of the distinctions. For example, progress is a value that is derived from the principles of potential and growth. Another distinction is the degree to which one can argue with a value, as compared to a principle. Twenty people can argue twenty different ways about the value called progress—What does progress look like? Is it progress if it doesn't improve something? Is it just technology or is it progress? and so on. Principles, on the other hand, are much more difficult to debate. Take potential and growth, for instance. People have potential and growth, plain and simple, just like rose bushes have potential to grow and produce blooms. We can argue about which color of rose is the most attractive, but we can't argue that rose bushes produce roses. Our choice about a principle is not about whether we accept it, but how we act upon it. We can nurture a principle or we can try to stifle it, but it will still be there no matter what we do.

Kiplinger's *America in the Global '90s* (1989) discussed the assault on American values and mores in the past twenty-five years. This period has been a time of unprecedented change and turbulence because of counterculture and drug explosions, the push for civil rights, a sexual revolution, the need to absorb the surge of women into the workplace, adjustment to high levels of immigration, and the explosive increases in teenage pregnancies, broken marriages, single-parent households, and latchkey children.

Our new informational society needs a set of values that

promotes interaction and understanding of the need for shared responsibility. An example of such a set includes

- the value of respect for property and each other's ideas;
- the value of character, integrity, honesty, honor, work, and creativity;
- the value of commitment and contributing to society;
- the value of shared responsibility for the stability of our families and neighborhoods;
- the value of nurturing and caring for all of our children in a nonthreatening environment by trained, responsible adults;
- the value of the highest quality of education by integrating the learning process through interaction with children and adults of different ages and at diverse levels of comprehension as the most competent way to learn how to solve problems and reach a higher level of learning, that is, comprehension, correlation, and synthesis.

As Mortimer J. Adler (1981, 150) stated in his book *Six Great Ideas* (which are truth, goodness, beauty, liberty, equality, and justice), "The only liberties to which we can make a claim upon society are the freedom to do as we please within the limits imposed by justice, and that is the political liberty enjoyed by enfranchised citizens of the republic."

Life has changed a lot since the days farmers needed their children for their physical strength as well as for their help with the endless chores of meal preparation, laundry, harvesting, and milking the cows. Farm life might have been rough and kids might not have had it all that easy, but the values were more clear: mutual respect, accomplishment, and shared responsibility. Children understood their set of values because they lived them every day. They saw them in action. It is difficult to miss the value of accomplishment when it means getting the crops in before they rot or the weather turns, and failure means hunger and possible loss of property.

Less than 4 percent of the population lives on farms today, and only 5 percent of the workforce works with the elements as do farmers, loggers, and fishers (*World* 1988, 814). Twenty million workers manufacture goods for some 220 million; the remaining 80 percent of workers provide services and manipulate symbols while exchanging information (Toffler 1981, 181).

The majority of these information exchangers rarely see the end result of their work. They frequently work alone at computers, having little communication with customers or other workers. Their rewards, if they are fortunate, are a good salary and job benefits. Their children have only a vague idea of what they do at work. Many adults, for that matter, are convinced that these information manipulators do inexplicable magic.

These days, 80 percent of the population crowds into sprawling metropolitan centers with almost no open space and few jobs that call for unskilled labor. Care for children who are forced to attend school only a few hours a day can become a financial burden. Or, children are left alone at home (hopefully) unattended, spending twice as much time watching television as they spend doing schoolwork. Two million latchkey kids go home to empty houses every day. Tens of thousands of children under the age of six stay at home alone all day (Packard 1983, 54). What set of values do they develop? If you ever feel that life seems to be becoming more and more like a soap opera, there may be a reason.

We've talked about the trend toward single-parent households. The roles of mothers and fathers, women and men generally, are becoming more blurred as women now hold the majority of professional jobs, formerly the domain of men (World 1988, 82). Parents, whether single or married, male or female, are trying to make a decent living, stay safe and healthy, maintain a home, be role models, teach values, be nurturing and loving. That's a lot to do.

"Not race, not income, but family structure offers the best

forecast of which children become criminals" (Berg 1993). That we continue to allow these single mothers to try to do everything alone is cause to examine our values with concern. The issue is not about "fixing it" for them, but to consider pooling our resources to share the responsibility for teaching their children values. The shift in perception required is not to make the people different. The shift in perception is to think of children as *our* future, *our* problem, *our* opportunity to share in their mastery of life.

Georgie Anne Geyer talked in the September 2, 1990, *Seattle Times* about pollster and analyst Daniel Yankelovich's comparison of values between 1950 and 1990. Yankelovich found our values had changed dramatically during that period. "The defining concerns went from production to consumption, from future to immediate, from sacrifice to greed, from public interest to self-interest, from quality to quantity, and from long-term to short-term."

Czech President Vaclav Havel believes that economic prosperity is not enough for a society. Civility and general cultural standards need to be raised as well. "We will never build a democratic state based on rule of law if we do not at the same time build a state that is humane, moral, intellectual and spiritual, and cultural" (Havel 1985).

Many organizations are trying to provide some of the missing elements of value education, but they can't do it all. Few families talk about values and goals. Our schools seldom give much importance to character development and values.

In the small town of Roswell, New Mexico, the community came together with a plan called Character-Counts, a grassroots effort of parents and teachers working together to teach their children a set of values. They chose words such as trustworthiness, caring, respect, justice, fairness, citizenship, kindness, consideration, and accountability.

Despite the fact that the town was far from the influence of any large urban area, teachers had noticed that their students had little respect for property and people, and much contempt for authority. The adults realized they had to be role models for their children by actively adopting these values in their daily lives. Each week the community emphasized one value. That value was posted in each classroom, every store and public building, and along the streets.

Teachers and students held discussions about fairness and how it affects individuals and the community. Clerks talked about the topic of the week with customers, the newspaper published letters, businesspeople held seminars with their employees, and families talked about the chosen subject during family meals.

This practice has brought the town together. Graffiti on buildings practically disappeared. Students demonstrate a new sense of self-respect and interest in learning.

Social support from the community has a great influence on the health and welfare of children. Studies have shown that communities with strong informal support networks and community involvement experienced less child abuse and neglect than a socially impoverished community.

Planning and talking about a change is necessary, but action helps keep motivation up among team members and momentum and enthusiasm at a peak. This is especially true of a really big project, such as taking back a neighborhood and creating a neighborhood campus. In the early stages, when planning is still in progress, there is one really useful question that can help: What can I (we) do right now?

What can each of us do right now to make some sort of difference in the lives of young children and teens? What demonstration of some value or values will provide a model for others? Addressing these questions is something you can always do on your own. If you're working with a team, talk about what you can be doing individually or as a group. Then do it, and afterward discuss the process and what happened.

Marian Wright Edelman wrote a short piece in the April 2, 1996, issue of *Family Circle* entitled "What Every Child Needs." She wrote, "It is time for us adults of every race and income group to break our silence about the pervasive breakdown of moral, family and community values, to place our children first in our lives, and to model the behavior we want our children to learn. Our 'youth problem' is not a youth problem, it is an adult problem, as our children do what they see us adults doing in our own lives. And they seek our attention in negative ways when we provide them too few positive ways to get the attention and love they need."

If we talk right and act wrong, according to Edelman, we are contributing to the crisis our children face. She suggests a personal audit to determine whether we are part of the solution or part of the problem. One area she suggests looking at: "If we think it's somebody else's responsibility to teach our children values, respect, polite manners and good work and health habits, we are part of the problem rather than the solution." (Edelman is founder and president of the Children's Defense Fund. Her latest book is *Guide My Feet*.)

Have you been a role model today? Being part of the solution doesn't have to be a big production or some heroic action. Living consistently with your values can mean, if you value kindness, giving someone a flower who's had a rough week at work. Living consistently with your values is more a function of awareness than of effort. The effort required is surprisingly minimal when you are aware of your values.

6
Practicing Shared Responsibility

＝⧓＝

No man is an Island, entire of itself, every man is a piece of the Continent,
a part of the main. Any man's death diminishes me, because I am involved in
Mankind; And therefore never send to know for whom the bell tolls;
it tolls for thee. —*John Donne*

One of the primary messages we keep coming back to throughout this discussion is that the family has shifted funda- mental loyalties as society has industrialized. People focus less on their responsibilities toward their kin and their families, and more on their desires for self-fulfillment as individuals (Robertson 1987, 355). Book after book and article after arti- cle address the trends resulting from this shift. The statistics tell us about those trends—in educational accomplishment, in the economic status of children and families, in the emotional and psychological toll on people—and they tell us what we need to do. There is no politically correct way to say what the numbers tell us—that children of single mothers, divorced or never married, are six times more likely to be poor than those living with two parents. They are more likely to suffer abuse or neglect and to do poorly in school. They are two to three times more likely to suffer emotional or behavioral problems.

They are more likely to abuse drugs, commit suicide, have babies as teenagers, and to go on welfare. They are more likely to have difficulty holding jobs and mates later in life, and more likely to commit crimes. And it's taking a risk to point out what the statistics tell us: three-fifths of black children are born to single mothers.

Rashida Jackson is twenty-four, a single mother of two, and had her first baby at thirteen. Now she teaches a course on sexual responsibility to middle-school students at the Afrocentric Educational Academy in Minneapolis. "Not talking openly about these things doesn't get anything solved," she said, acknowledging that whites have long avoided the subject for fear of being branded racists or antifeminists. Blacks, too, have avoided it for fear of accusations from other blacks that sexual responsibility means genocide. "What I say is look around you. . . . a twelve-year-old girl and boy going to have a child? *That's* genocide. People are going to have to start saying what they really believe and take the risk of being called a racist or a sexist because some things are worth the risk—our children" (Berg 1993).

As we focused on self-fulfillment, the quality of education disintegrated to such a degree that two-thirds of people in remedial programs for basic subjects (math, reading, and comprehension) are high school graduates. One of the most educated generations ever, the baby boomers, has created a legacy of poor education. In our quest to fulfill ourselves individually, we have failed to pass on values to the next generation. A generation that so cautiously approaches war as a political option has left a wake of domestic and social violence.

Still, it's almost taboo to suggest that the source of these problems might be cultural, rather than just economic. Steve Berg (1993) wrote: "It has been conventional for serious analysts and mainline politicians to accept these changes in family structure as inevitable or, in some cases, as a desirable rebellion against the oppressions of past forms. Any adverse consequences for children—poverty, for example—have been blamed largely on the economy, specifically the well-documented diminishing income prospects of the past twenty years."

Berg continued by asking if economic stress is really the most important reason that, for example, so many men flee their parental responsibilities. Is it sadly possible that the nation suffers an excess of tolerance that creates a lethal partnership between bad economy and bad culture? David Blankenhorn, director of the Institute for American Values in New York, says yes.

"Better education and better jobs would help," Berg quoted Blankenhorn as saying. "But it's also true that man, for example, lives in a world that does not tell him that a good man, irrespective of his circumstance, does not ignore his obligation to his child and so he doesn't have a cultural idea in his head about what it means to be a father. And so we also have a cultural problem."

Just as no single teenage mother is responsible for the trends we're seeing that affect children, neither is any single one of us responsible as we continue to strive for self-fulfillment. What we see is the cost of forgetting that each one of us does make a difference, and not always in a positive way. When enough of us put ourselves first, without thinking of the impact of our actions on others—our families, our neighborhoods, and our country—we find ourselves with a bit of a mess. There is nothing inherently wrong with self-fulfillment; on a personal level, taking care of ourselves is necessary before taking care of others. Our expectations, however, that we must first take care of ourselves completely and totally before looking around are unrealistic.

There is no definitive argument that will convince every individual that what we must do is reclaim the value named "service to others." We can continue to talk about the costs of all these problems to each of us, whether in the form of taxes to pay for welfare or the personal loss we suffer as a result of crime or suicide or depression or substance abuse, and it won't have an effect. No one can convince any of us that we need to take action by saying we should do so "because it's good for you," as some of our mothers used to tell us. Likewise, we're not going to fall for the line "you messed it up, now you fix it," because we have spent so much time in our quest for self-ful-fillment that we now know that no one should be able to tell us what to do.

The only worthwhile appeal is that we should do some-thing because we can. We share in the responsibility for the state of circumstances eroding our children's well-being; we can share in the responsibility for improving those circum-stances. The appeal is not just economic, it is also cultural; it is an appeal to values and principles. It is a request that we become principle-centered, as Covey says. The authors assume that if you are reading this book, you are willing to respond to the request. Therefore, we don't have to discuss the reasons why you should or shouldn't any further. You know the reasons or you are willing to find them. So now the focus becomes how we can share responsibility for reclaiming our values, our children, and our neighborhoods.

Taking back our neighborhoods and building communities that work require the following steps:

1. understanding the history of social structures and how that history has affected what we see today;

2. understanding the reasons for poverty, how it affects your family, and how you can help eliminate it;

3. setting up a set of values and goals that your family understands and accepts, and living by them;

4. changing your thinking from egocentric independence to shared responsibility, and thinking in terms of human ecol-ogy.

We've laid the groundwork for the first three steps. Let's continue to explore the last step. The vitality of a neighbor-hood and the stability of the family are interdependent. The weakening bonds of a family affect everyone living in a neigh-borhood. When children of a disrupted family go out of their homes into the neighborhood, they take their pain and anger with them. They vent their frustrations in the neighborhood, the results of which include vandalism, destruction of property, and violence toward other people, their neighbors.

The actions we can take fall into two broad categories: social action and personal action. For the purposes of this discussion, social action represents action we all take as a society, such as supporting welfare. Personal action includes what we can do as individuals, families, neighborhoods, and other groups smaller than the entire society.

Social Action—Possibilities for Change

In one sense, that we have a concern for sharing responsibility for our present situation is evident in the fact that all of us who pay taxes support the welfare system. Debatable is whether the system in place actually improves the lot of those who must use it. This debate has a long history and most likely a long future life. There are two things we can consider here: that our support of some social system of aid still leaves us personally distanced from sharing responsibility for change, and that there may be alternatives to the present welfare system that might make it more effective.

The Minneapolis *Star Tribune* ran a three-part series of articles by Jean Hopfensperger (1996) comparing the welfare system in the United States to that in Western European countries. Whereas the welfare system in the United States concentrates on the poor single parent, in most European countries all families are assisted with free preschool, health insurance, nursing care in their homes when needed, and a monthly allowance for each child in each family to help buy food, clothes, and other necessities. If one of the parents is unable to provide financial support for the children after divorce, the government pays a stipend to the custodial parent. Elizabeth Lion of the French Ministry of Social Affairs and Health said,

"The idea is that all children should have the same rights, and those rights should be independent of the income of the parents."

In the United States, when a single mother takes a full-time job she loses all welfare benefits including health insurance. If she works at the lower end of the pay scale, she is unable to pay for daycare for her children. American two-parent families have only recently become eligible for aid, another factor that further threatens otherwise stable families.

In Europe, low- and middle-class families receive housing allowances; in the United States, only the poorest of families receive vouchers or rent subsidies to live in government-owned housing projects. A single parent in France is allowed about $460 a month for one child under the age of three. After that age, the child attends one of the free government preschools found in many of the neighborhoods, freeing the parent to work without worrying about childcare. After birth, infants have access to good preventive healthcare at the neighborhood health clinic. Social and financial counselors are at the center to give aid where it is needed. Midwives and nurses visit homes when necessary.

In the city of Lyon, France, there are 145 health clinics that keep records on 30,000 children under the age of two. "The key is to set up shop where the people live," said Maryse Vocanson, regional director of the program.

At least twenty other European countries have lower infant mortality rates than the United States. In fact, the US has the highest child poverty rate of any major Western industrialized nation; the widest gap between rich and poor families of those nations; the highest teen pregnancy rate; and an infant mortality rate that is higher than nineteen Western nations, including Spain and Greece; and a larger percentage of babies born at low birth weights than thirty other nations.

After Laos fell to Communist rule in the mid-1970s, a group of families sharing the same ancestry immigrated to two places—Minnesota and France. A comparison of these Hmong immigrants revealed a number of differences between the families that ended up in Minnesota and those that ended up in France.

While both groups arrived in their respective countries with few marketable skills and little grasp of the language and culture, "the vast majority of the Hmong in France have been holding jobs since they arrived." The Hmong in Minnesota, on the other hand, have the highest welfare use among Minnesota's immigrants. Hmong leaders attribute the difference to France's system of child allowances, family childcare options, and work disincentives built into the US welfare system.

Lyxuxu Lyfoung, a leader of the French Hmong community who has visited Minnesota, said, "A big advantage in France is we have the family allowance. For example, if you're pregnant, the government helps you [financially] from the first month until you deliver the baby. After that you get the child allowance. And you can work if you get it. In the US, if the family is on welfare, they can't work. It seems like if you work, you earn less money than if you are on welfare."

The French have enviable childcare programs that clearly enable parents to work. They have the *école maternal*, a public preschool that is mandatory for three-year-olds. There are the after-school daycare centers that take children to other government-certified childcare centers until late-working parents can pick them up.

One other advantage of the French childcare network, and particularly *les écoles maternals*, is that it levels the intellectual and developmental playing field for poor and rich children of immigrants and native-born French. Nearly 54 percent of unskilled workers' children who have not spent time in nursery school have to repeat first grade. That compares with 38 percent who have attended two years of preschool.

The French system has been expensive. "Overall spending on child well-being is $229 billion in France, compared with $146 billion in the United States." Olga Baudelot, senior researcher at France's National Center of Pedological Research, pointed out that "in the US, there is excellent daycare, but you have to have money to use it. In France, it's part of our integration model." Lyfoung said, "The French government has a longer-term vision than the US. If you pay for kids when they are young, they will pay taxes when they are older."

The "Eurowelfare" series continued examining the social programs worldwide. "More than eighty countries have 'child allowances'; more than one hundred countries offer *paid* maternity leave; every industrialized nation besides South Africa has national health insurance; and every country in Europe has or is planning preschool care, according to studies by Professor Sheila Kammerman, codirector of the Cross-National Studies Research Program at Columbia University."

These programs indicate a philosophy of promoting shared responsibility; in Europe they are considered an investment in the future stability and well-being of a nation. In the US, on the other hand, social benefits often are considered an intrusion into families or business, or a step toward socialism.

Neither the American nor the European systems are without faults as well as benefits. The European programs are expensive, which makes labor very expensive as well, particularly after the cost of the social package is added to wages. For this reason and others, many countries in Europe are looking at aspects of our program, while we in turn are trying some of their ideas. More than twenty states are experimenting with German-style apprenticeship programs for high school and technical students. "In schools and nurseries in thirty states, three- and four-year-olds are attending public preschools that look a lot like . . . the French public preschools. And pregnant women at risk of poor deliveries are getting home nurse visits and prenatal care in cities from Baltimore to San Diego, sparked in part by health officials' visits to France."

Many other interesting programs seem to work in other countries, and parts of programs here in the US work. Perhaps one of the most effective actions we can take is to learn about these options, and take our knowledge to the voting booths.

Personal Action—
Making a Positive Difference

If we consider that the community belongs to the individual, and we are determined that individuals can and do make a difference, then we can start change at home. Everyone from newborn infants to seniors can benefit, and there is no need to change any governmental agencies or departments at this level of participation. The possibility exists for every person living in a neighborhood to be connected through a center that offers something of value, value as determined by the people themselves. The idea of the neighborhood campus puts services like daycare, healthcare, recreation, and education right there near our own front doors—and under our direct control.

As Aburdene and Naisbitt (1992) noted, "Traditionally, America's housewives were the backbone of organizations seeking justice in an unjust world. In the fifties, sixties, even into the seventies, women from all income groups put volunteering high on their list of priorities. But as women joined the work force, volunteering suffered. The 'me generation' took the blame: selfish yuppies, even women, were out to take care of 'number one.'" Given that women starting out in the business world of the 1970s had to prove their competence, maybe there is some truth to this accusation of self-absorption. Many probably did have to work twice as hard as male colleagues. A number of other areas like family, marriage, and friendship also suffered as devotion to career became an exclusive relationship.

"But," Aburdene and Naisbitt continued, "in the 1990s the desire to contribute has reemerged at home and in the office. Women are concerned about a long list of issues, and working women are confident enough on the job to embrace a new priority—service."

Taking Back Our Neighborhoods

We have demonstrated—men, too—that we do want to take personal action to share the responsibility for making our country a place that works for everyone. The logical next question is, What if we take that action in our own neighborhoods?

At the same time we improve our knowledge and exercise our right to vote for better options at the level of social action, each person can become an active participant in managing the social services within each neighborhood. The bigger picture is extremely important, but the scope of that picture makes it difficult to discern the difference one person makes in the change process. The more focused picture in the neighborhood allows the deeply satisfying value of each person's contribution to shine in rich detail.

The neighborhood campus proposes to foster shared responsibility between government agencies, families, and individuals in neighborhoods. The goal is to help people help themselves, to empower people to solve their own problems.

The May 11, 1989, issue of *Time* included an article entitled "On the Front Lines" by Richard La Cayo. La Cayo reported numerous examples of neighbors sharing responsibility for the safety and welfare of their community. In South Philadelphia, for example, neighbors formed the Twentieth and Tasker Improvement Council after a stray bullet fired during a feud between drug dealers paralyzed a six-year-old boy. The council's goal was to "get people out from behind their closed doors." The neighbors, in groups of two or more, patrolled their neighborhood each night. They stood conspicuously on street corners and wrote down the license numbers of cars that drove slowly along the street. The cars and the drug dealers left.

The New Orleans Velocity Foundation set up twenty-two drug-free zones around the city. After Los Angelenos formed the Brotherhood Crusade Black United Fund, crime "dropped 67 percent in a thirty-six block area that had been patrolled by the group in just one month." In Chicago, a parish priest led a campaign to stop the sale of drug paraphernalia in neighbor-hood candy stores. In Berkeley, the Francisco Street Community Group brought court action against a landlord of a crack house, and the tenant was evicted. The Stella Link Revitalization Coalition, a group of Houston civic associations from nine area neighborhoods with a population of 20,000, was able to clean up derelict buildings to make drug-free apartment houses.

Patrollers in Providence, Rhode Island, collect details such as car license numbers and descriptions of people passing money or drugs. In New York City, community patrol officers work with neighborhood organizers. Belle Meade in Miami put barriers across five of six streets that lead into an area where drug dealing was rampant. While Miami averaged an 11 percent increase in crime last year, Belle Meade's area declined 16 percent. Like Kimi Gray, Belle Meade took the initiative to bring about change in her neighborhood. As she told the reporter, "Someone has to make the difference. If you don't start with yourself, it will never get done."

These are just a few illustrations of ways individuals have worked together in neighborhoods to bring about change. Through cooperation and interaction, neighbors are discovering that the concept of shared responsibility works in their neighborhoods. They are also discovering that shared responsibility works for them personally as they boost their self-esteem, sense of belonging, and personal identity.

That's how you can take back your neighborhood and make it work.

Two Families:
How the Neighborhood
Campus Can Work

⋟⊦ ⊦⋞

It is July 31, and we're on the set of *You Don't Say* with Andie Smith Ramirez, your talk show host. Joining Andie today are Dr. Myra Moore, sociologist; Jane and Ted Mansfield, with their children Marcia and Malcolm; and Ann and Bob Sanders and their children, Jon, Sara, and Tim. This is the third in a series entitled "Families Today: Values, Concerns, and Interests." Please note that the television show and host and all guests are purely fictional.

Andie: Welcome, everybody. We're here today with two pretty typical families to help us take a look at where our families are today in America. Yesterday we talked with Paula and Joanna, two single moms, about what they face raising their kids in the inner city. Monday we talked to Melissa and Paul—Melissa, an unwed teenage mother, and Paul, a single dad, caring for his two young children since his wife was tragically killed in a robbery at a neighborhood convenience store.

So today we'll be talking with two families—Jane and Ted and Ann and Bob and their children—who represent families pretty much like yours out there in TV land. Also joining us is Dr. Myra Moore. Dr. Moore is a sociologist whose special interest is today's families and the impact of social trends on young people. Dr. Moore is the author of *What's Up: Boomers and the Turn of the Century, Gen X Is Alive and Well on Planet Y,* and most recently, *The Addictive Internet: Coping in a Virtual World.* Thank you all for being here today.

Let's start with you, Jane and Ted. Tell us about yourselves. Jane?

Jane: Well, Andie, I guess we're pretty typical, as you said. Let's see, Ted works in a computer components manufacturing plant. He's a manager there. I work out in the tech center. I'm a supervisor for customer service in a telecommunications company. Um, these are our kids. Marcia here is six, and Malcolm is eighteen months. (Jane bounces the baby on her lap. Ted sits quietly, smiling.)

Andie: Ted, what do you do with the kids while you work? Are you having trouble with daycare or school or anything like that? We hear so much about that these days.

Ted: (Ted shifts in his seat, frowning slightly as he considers the question.) We've got Malcolm in a daycare center. I don't know, I guess it's okay. Marcia just started first grade this year. They seem okay. Jane, are we having any problems with that stuff?

Jane: (Jane shifts Malcolm to her other arm, setting her mouth firmly as she shoots an angry look at Ted.) As a matter of fact, I'm not very happy with the daycare center. I mean, it's okay. They take pretty good care of Malcolm and all. It's just too far away, and we pay so much for it and I don't think they really do anything with the kids. I mean, it seems like with all the money we spend on it that they should be teaching the kids something. Anyway, it's a pain, but I can't do anything about it. Marcia's school is okay. I have to take her to a different daycare center. They have a bus that takes her to school from there, and brings her back after school in the afternoon. I don't know what they do with Marcia at her daycare center in the afternoons. She doesn't talk about it much, but it seems okay.

Andie: What about Marcia's school?

Jane: Well, it's supposed to be a pretty good school. It's not real close to our house, but it has a good reputation and all. Marcia seems to like it pretty well. You know, she's reading a little now, and brings home lots of drawings.

Andie: Okay. What about you, Ann and Bob? Now, you guys are a little older, right? But your children, except for Tim, are around the same ages as Malcolm and Marcia. Is your story pretty much the same?

Bob: Yes and no. Generally, I think our jobs are all more or less similar, except Ann and I both work downtown. And yes, we are a little older, but not that much. Tim is my son from my first marriage. Ann and I had Jon and Sara after we got married. Tim's mother travels a lot with her job, so Tim lives with us most of the time. Let's see, Tim's thirteen, Jon is seven, Sara's four, I'm forty-eight, and I always let Ann tell her own age so I don't get in trouble.

Ann: (Laughing. Sara has been a little restless, and Ann has been talking to her quietly to calm her.) I just turned forty, Andie. I don't mind telling.

Andie: It's a good year, isn't it? I loved forty. So, is your life pretty much like Jane and Ted's so far?

Ann: In some ways, but there are differences. When we were talking before the show, Jane and Ted said they live in a newer neighborhood in their city. Bob and I decided we wanted to be in an older part of town so we could be closer to work. And we just wanted those nice big old trees and maybe a park nearby. We have kind of a neat thing, though, and it works out really well since it lets us take the bus to work, so we only have to have one car. We have a neighborhood campus in our area.

Andie: Okay, now tell us about that. It sounded pretty interesting when I read about it before the show.

Bob: We're all—all of us in our neighborhood—still working on it, but so far it's great. What we did was take the elementary school and make it into a combination community center, daycare and school facility, and a place for the kids and adults to hang out. See, a couple of years ago, we had some trouble with one of the houses not too far from ours. A lot of our neighbors are pretty much like us, but since we're in an older neighborhood, we also have a lot of older folks. And we have some old homes that have been made into apartments. Those have younger single people—some young single mothers, and some guys that share places while they're in the med school or at the university downtown. Anyway, a bunch of young kids had pretty much taken over one of those apartment houses, and it turned out they were dealing drugs.

Ann: But there's also the poorer area a couple of blocks away. We're in one of those neighborhoods where for some reason part stayed pretty nice over the years—a little rundown, but basically nice—but just a few blocks away it became pretty raggedy. That area has a lot of rental houses, and the people who live there are relatively transient. So some of those kids were coming over to buy drugs from the guys in that house, and we were seeing a lot of graffiti, vandalism, and trash left lying around. Sometimes it was pretty scary. We've gotten to know a lot of people in that area now, and they're mostly nice folks. In fact, it's really interesting to talk to many of them. But it's the nature of that part of the neighborhood. Since it's mostly rental houses and people move in and out a lot, there's not much reason for them to care about keeping up the neighborhood.

Bob: So anyway, the kids in those apartments got busted one day. And again not long after, but that time the police had to shoot a guy. Then one of the kids, a little girl, was shot in a drive-by shooting. Everybody was pretty upset and scared, and several families started talking about moving.

Andie: It seems like that kind of thing is happening all over. So what did you do?

Ann: Well, we didn't want to move. We really believe people can make a difference anyway, so we kept talking to people about staying and making the neighborhood safe. We'd

94

read this book about setting up a neighborhood campus, and we started talking to people about doing that in our area. We like the people, we want Sara and Jon and Tim to know lots of different people with different backgrounds, and we want all of us to be safe.

Andie: Okay, so you wanted to stay but you wanted things to be different. Isn't that a bit unrealistic? Dr. Moore, can you tell us about this neighborhood campus thing?

Dr. Moore: Andie, it's not unrealistic to believe people can make things different where they live. In fact, more and more families are becoming fed up with living in fear and at the mercy, if you will, of people who just don't value life and property. A lot of us are getting back in touch with our desire, need even, for close relationships with people who live around us. People used to get that from their families when families used to stay together for generations. Now we have to look for that sense of belonging in the people we end up living around, to create our own extended families, in a sense.

Andie: Right, I get that. But people don't know each other anymore. (Andie looks out at the studio audience.) Do ya'll know your neighbors? I don't . . . well, some of them. How do you get a bunch of people you don't know together to do something like this?

Dr. Moore: Pretty much like Ann and Bob have. You start talking to people about doing something. True, somebody has to come up with a vision, with a clear picture of what they want the change to be like. But anyone can do that, and once it's clear, then other people can see it, too. It sounds like Ann and Bob started the vision in their neighborhood, right?

Bob: Yes, I guess we did. We didn't think about it that way, though. In fact, we didn't really have a clue about how we were going to change things. We just knew we weren't going to put up with things the way they were anymore. And like Ann said, we'd read this book and we thought we could make it work. The more we talked to people about it, the more they got interested in making a neighborhood campus, too.

Taking Back Our Neighborhoods

Andie: Ted, Jane—do you guys have anything like this?

Jane: I still don't know what it is, but we don't know very many people around us except for the people right next door and right across the street. I haven't heard about any kind of campus thing. Everybody's so busy, and things seem pretty calm and safe around us. The kids get a little out of hand sometimes, but it's mostly just kid stuff.

Dr. Moore: The neighborhood campus idea, Andie, is a way for people to take back the management of their schools and really, their lives. The campus is usually the neighborhood elementary school, and the residents redesign its functions so that it becomes more or less a center where everyone in the community can take advantage of daycare, school, parent and adult classes, a senior center, all kinds of activities, plus health services and a crisis center. Those are usually the basic components.

Andie: Now that sounds pretty amazing, like too good to be true.

Ann: We thought that, too, at first. But once you get started, it pretty much falls together. It is a lot of work, but it's really been a lot of fun, too. We got people to talk to all the different social services places, like the Parks and Recreation Department and the education people. We had to do a lot of planning, but there are so many people in the neighborhood that know people or know how to get different things done. Everybody had to work at it, but the more people who got involved, the more we all spread the work out. And we've got just about everything Dr. Moore mentioned. We're still working on some of the parenting classes, and the arts and recreation center can use some more activities. But we've got a good start on it.

Andie: Okay, let's look at something else here. Ted, you guys don't have anything like this. So let's compare. Tell us about a typical day for you, then we'll ask Ann and Bob the same thing. I want to know how this campus really is different.

Ted: Well, we get up pretty early. Jane has to get the kids ready, and I vanpool to work and that's about an hour and a half. Plus we, the vanpool gang, usually have breakfast on the way. Jane feeds the kids and takes them to their daycare places.

Jane: Yeah, Ted rides happily to work with his friends. I get to drive through rush hour traffic to two different daycare centers, plus I have to make sure both kids have all their stuff. And they really hate it at the centers if we're late. Then I have to make sure I have all my stuff together, and try to get to my office on time. I probably just lost a promotion because I was late again yesterday.

Ted: Jane, you know I'd help if I could. I can't help it that the company assigned me to the plant way out there. Anyway, then we work all day. Jane and the kids are home when I get home, but I'm usually so late that the kids have already eaten. We all watch TV. Sometimes I'll have a nap when I get home while Jane does stuff. That's about it.

Jane: That "stuff" I do is take care of the kids' "stuff" and the house "stuff." I can't get home late and take a nap. I have to leave work no matter what's going on to make sure I get the kids from daycare on time, because they charge an ungodly amount of money if they have to keep them any extra time. And then there's seeing what they did in school, or laundry, and I try to play with them a little. I have to fix dinner, and when I was working on my master's degree I had to study, too. I don't know where that time went that I used to have to spend studying. It seems like I still just rush all day long. I don't know how anybody has time to set up some campus deal. What are you guys—Mr. and Mrs. Perfectly Organized? (Jane leans over to look at Ann and Bob.)

Ann: (Ann seems a little perplexed by Jane's tone.) No, well, I guess we are pretty well organized. We don't think about it that much. I used to have to do what you do, but it's so different now. One of us just walks the kids over to the campus in the morning, or some of the families take turns driving them over if the weather's bad. And we helped write the curriculum, so we know the kids are learning what we want them to learn.

Bob: You know, we have to spend some time working at the campus. We use it, so we help support it. But I doubt we spend any more time working at the campus, or taking the courses in parenting that we agree to keep up with, than we used to spend running around.

Andie: Jane or Ted, what do you guys do for fun? Do you have any fun?

Ted: (He and Jane look at each other.) I guess we go out sometimes, usually to dinner with friends or we'll go to a cocktail party. Sometimes we go to a movie, usually with the kids. Sometimes on the weekend I go play golf or basketball with some of my friends from work.

Jane: We just don't have time. And if we did, we can't really afford to go out all that much. We have a nice house, and nice clothes. The kids always have what they need. But it takes both of us working to make it, with the mortgage and daycare.

Andie: What about you guys?

Ann: We do a lot more now, actually, than we used to as a family, even though we don't really go out that much. There's always something going on over at the campus. And the kids either want to be there, or the nice older lady down the street will watch them if Bob and I want to go out. We usually have a "date" once a week. I guess about once a week we go do something with the children, like a movie or go to the funplex. Tim has football and baseball, so most of the year we have his games to go to. He plays on the teams at the campus, too, in the after-school program, so we do that with all the neighbors. We'll all usually do a picnic on the weekends after or before the game. Let's see, Sara starts dance lessons next week in the after-school program. And Jon is already interested in the theater workshops there, so we'll be going to their recitals and plays.

Bob: We almost always have coffee and pie with some of the other parents after parenting class every week. And we both have friends we've met who work over at the campus at the same times we do. So we have lots of time alone, alone with each other, and with other parents and their families. We've even gotten to know, like Ann said, some of the people that rent in the area over a few blocks. A couple of people who have become friends are single, but they're both at the campus a lot, too, especially for the singles groups. One's from Korea—she's going to school at the university—and she comes over fairly often to play with Jon and Sara. The other guy we spend some time with has a family in Mexico City, so we have him over for holidays and dinner so he doesn't have to be alone. We have our friend, the older lady Ann mentioned, for holiday meals, too.

Ann: It's funny, because you just get used to having so much to do right there at home and so many neat people, that it's hard to remember sometimes what a hassle it used to be to go do anything.

Jane: I'd love to be able to take a class or two. I've always wanted to learn to paint. I just don't see how I could take the time right now. (She looks over at Ted again.)

Andie: So it sounds like this neighborhood campus has helped with more than just daycare and school. Dr. Moore, are there enough neighborhoods that have done this sort of thing that you know what impact it's having on people?

Dr. Moore: There are more and more efforts like, if not the same as, the neighborhood campus. In these kinds of communities, we generally find that people are more secure. They feel safer and consider themselves generally happier than people in families that are relatively isolated emotionally from others. They tend to spend more time in social activities as a family. It will be interesting to watch this sort of movement over the next few years.

Andie: You bring up a good point, Dr. Moore. (He looks around at the group.) How would you rate your overall satisfaction with your lifestyles? Are you happy? Ted, how about you?

Ted: I haven't really thought about it much, but I guess I'm pretty satisfied. I don't know anything that's really wrong with the way we live. I guess I'm pretty happy.

Jane: It's okay, but I just keep wondering if this is all there is. I mean, I've got a family and a career and we do okay, but it just seems like we shouldn't have to always be scrambling to get somewhere or to get the money together to pay bills. I'm okay with things, I guess. Happy? Yeah, I suppose I'm happy.

Andie: What about you, Bob and Ann?

Bob: I'm real happy. Sure, I'd like to go to Europe and build a state-of-the-art workshop in the backyard, but I really love our lifestyle.

Ann: Me, too. I think the only thing I'd do different is work at home, and maybe pretty soon I can figure out a way to do that. I like my job, but I need to work right now, too, like Jane does. Well, like most of us do. But everything just seems to be working out the way I've always hoped it would. Bob and I are happy with each other, our kids are happy and healthy. Yeah. I'm very happy.

Andie: Dr. Moore, did you want to say something else?

Dr. Moore: Yes, Andie. One of the things we've learned is that the more clear people are about their values—especially as a family—the more they seem to be able to find happiness for themselves. Or at least to feel satisfied, no matter what their circumstances. My guess is that Jane and Ted don't talk much about values, what they believe in, and I'd bet that Bob and Ann do.

Andie: What about that, guys? Jane?

Jane: I'm not sure what you mean. I mean, we talk about money and school and the kids. What people are doing, things like that. Our family is important to us, but we don't talk about it much.

Andie: What about you, Ted? What's your take on that?

Ted: Well, Jane's right. We don't talk about stuff like that much. It doesn't seem like a big deal, because a value isn't going to put dinner on the table.

Bob: Actually, Ted, I disagree. Hard work and persistence, feeling responsible for the well-being of your family, caring—those things put dinner on the table, and they're values. You and Jane obviously have those values.

Andie: Do you and Ann talk about values, Bob?

Bob: We do. In fact, before we decided to move to where we are now, we all sat down—the kids, too—and talked about what's important to us. Tim threw a few things on the table, but Jon and Sara were a little young to really contribute. We knew a move would change things for us, especially since we didn't own our own house before.

Ann: We wanted Jon and Sara to at least be part of the discussion, even if they couldn't participate that much. And Tim had some really good things to contribute. He said it was really important to him to have friends and to play ball, so he didn't care where we moved, as long as we were all together and he could do those things. Bob and I had to look at where we placed our work in our value system. We both felt work was important, but our family was more important. So we made a list of the sort of things to look for in a new home that would best support what we wanted for all of us. Bob turned down a promotion that would have meant spending a lot of time at the main division of his company, which is clear across the country. It would have meant enough additional money that I probably wouldn't have had to keep working, but when we looked at everything all together, the way we've done it has been the best. And you know, working with people to start the neighborhood campus has given me, and Bob, too, I think, some other career options. Some day I might like to go around and help other neighborhoods do this, maybe after the kids are in college.

Andie: Well, we're out of time now. I want to thank all of you again for being here today. (Andie turns to the camera.) Tomorrow we'll meet a widow who is a senior citizen living alone, and a retired couple raising their young grandchildren. Until then, take care.

7
The Neighborhood Campus Board

Capability is like a water table below the surface of the earth. No one owns it, but you can tap it. —Katagiri Roshi

This chapter is the beginning of the plan that you can use as a model for creating a neighborhood campus of your own. When we use "you" in this and the following chapters, read the word as it fits your circumstances. If you are an individual who wants to mobilize others in your community to bring a neighborhood campus into reality, then obviously read "you" to mean yourself. Otherwise, if you're already working with a group of your neighbors to make the campus happen, then "you" refers to all of you serving as leaders for the project.

To make this part of the book as useful as possible, we'll first approach the guidelines from the standpoint that you'll be working under ideal circumstances. That way, you can use the information to continue clarifying your vision and detailing in your imagination how the process will work. Of course, the same information serves as an outline, which can be tailored to your specific needs. Later in each chapter, we'll offer some practical suggestions for effective implementation. You are the most qualified to anticipate how people in your neighborhood will respond to the creation of a neighborhood campus, so we'll give you as much basic information as we can to enable you to deal with a variety of circumstances.

You may have noticed in the brief stories of people making changes in their communities that many who have been successful did not necessarily have any experience in what they did. You don't have to have any special training; all you really need is desire, commitment, patience, willingness to learn, and willingness to ask people for help when you need it.

At times you may feel the outlines for development of the neighborhood campus board and the various centers are somewhat vague. They are. There is no way to address the needs of every neighborhood and what each resident will expect from the neighborhood campus. These outlines are exactly that: outlines.

However, Dr. Thomas Gordon (1980) said something interesting in his book *Leadership Effectiveness Training*: "My experience as a consultant to organizations convinces me that most leaders greatly underestimate the wealth of knowledge, ideas, and ingenuity lying untapped in the heads of group members." With an open framework, the knowledge, research, and creativity of the groups or teams that you'll be forming will fill in the gaps so that your plan will be perfectly suited to your neighborhood.

Tom Peters and Robert Waterman (1982) studied some of the most successfully managed companies for their book, *In Search of Excellence*. One of the not-so-secret pieces of information they found was that "small groups are, quite simply, the basic organizational building blocks of excellent companies." They found a remarkable correlation between effective teams in excellent companies and the best academic findings about the makeup of effective small groups. "For instance," they reported, "the effective productivity or new product teams in the excellent companies usually range from five to ten in size. The academic evidence is clear on this: optimal group size, in most studies, is about seven." In addition, "teams that consist of *volunteers,* are of *limited duration,* and *set their own goals* are usually found to be much more productive." So, the ideal size of a team or group is important, but equally important is the similarity between groups working within a company and groups in any setting working to achieve a goal. The key elements are that volunteers with limited tenure who set their own goals are most effective.

In *Teaching the Elephant to Dance,* Belasco (1990) talked about Jack Welch, chief executive officer of General Electric. Welch, an expert in producing change, said, "We have found what we believe to be the distilled essence of competitiveness. It is the reservoir of talent and creativity and energy that can be found in each of our people. That essence is liberated when we make people believe that what they think and do is important—and then get out of their way while they do it." Other than the fact that you're not competing, Welch's words pretty well summarize the basic philosophy of an effective leader.

The Neighborhood Campus Board: The Ideal Model

The neighborhood campus has a neighborhood campus board, which is responsible for the operation of the campus. Ideally, the board (or leadership team) will consist of representatives from two-parent families, one-parent families, singles, seniors, professionals who work with the children in the neighborhood school, and children over the age of ten. The number of representatives from each category should reflect the proportion of each in your community. For example, if there are fifty two-parent families in a neighborhood of one hundred residents, that category would have five members on a ten-person board, or one representative for every ten families or individuals.

The children are a category by themselves for the purpose of this count, regardless of their family status. The children who are on the board represent students in the neighborhood, rather than the groups determined by their family structures.

The neighborhood campus board is responsible for budget, administration, personnel, maintenance, goals, adoption of a set of values and disciplinary procedures, and curricula for all centers on the campus. One of the board's first duties is to choose a representative for the city school board.

A reasonable term for each board member is four years, except for child representatives who will serve for one year. Each representative receives a fair salary appropriate to the task he or she assumes. Some research will yield information about salaries in your area for the different positions.

Every board member should expect to spend time working in each of the neighborhood campus centers so that he or she understands how each center functions. This practice of rotating through all the functional areas also allows board members to see how the different centers fit into the operation of the campus as a whole.

All social, health, and human needs services continue to operate as they have through their respective agencies and organizations. The only difference is the location of their professional staff, who now work at each neighborhood campus instead of the agency or organization offices. The number of workers at the neighborhood campus depends on the demographic distribution in the neighborhood. These workers are considered part of the campus staff and are represented on the campus board. All receive salaries commensurate with training, experience, and working hours. Each agency or organization involved allocates funds for salaries and operating expenses of the neighborhood campus.

The neighborhood campus operates throughout the year. The elementary school, or learning center, is also open year-round. The school operates in ten-week quarters with vacation periods between quarters. The individual centers operate continuously. Because working parents depend upon the daycare and after-school recreation centers, those teachers, workers, and administrators plan their vacations on a revolving basis.

It is necessary to restructure the neighborhood elementary school to start a neighborhood campus. One suggestion: consider a model similar to a charter school in planning this restructuring, amended with provisions for the establishment of the neighborhood campus.

In the past few years, there has been a growing movement toward charter schools. Minnesota started the movement in 1991; today eleven states have passed laws permitting their establishment. These schools offer the best hope thus far of offering our children a higher quality education. The advantages of charter schools are that they are free to spend their allotted money as they see fit, and they allow for experimentation, creativity, and inclusion of parents as equal partners in the education process. Their disadvantages are that they take money away from the already failing public schools, and they are not required to have a collective bargaining agreement with the teachers' unions.

The best possibility of the charter school model lies in restructuring the neighborhood elementary school, in which the teachers likely already have collective bargaining. The neighborhood campus can use the laws set up for charter schools to start the campus, thus avoiding legal entrapments (Wallis 1994, 53–56).

Such a restructuring will require the full support of all the neighborhood residents, not just the parents of school-age children. Everyone in the community has the opportunity to benefit from the neighborhood campus, but only if everyone shares responsibility for its development and maintenance.

Practical Suggestions for Implementing the Neighborhood Campus Board

One secret for successful management of any project is to stay clear about your vision, but also deal with reality. Initially, follow the structure outlined above in planning your board, and then adapt that to fit your particular needs as you continue your research.

We can't emphasize enough the necessity for clearly defined values. A practical way to define the values you want to adopt as you create your neighborhood campus is to write a mission statement. Appendix A contains Stephen Covey's (1994) outline of a mission statement workshop from his book *First Things First.* He also suggests that an empowering organizational mission statement

- focuses on contribution, on worthwhile purposes that create a collective, passionate "Yes!" from organization members;
- comes from the bowels of the organization, not from Mount Olympus;
- is based on timeless principles;
- contains both vision and principle-based values;
- addresses the needs of all stakeholders.

A very simple method for creating a set of values and a mission statement is to have all the representatives and as many residents as possible attend a values meeting. As people call out values they want to see become integrated into the neighborhood campus, have someone write them on a large chalkboard, whiteboard, or a piece of poster board. Whether the board members then consolidate these values into a mission statement for presentation to the group at large, or a task force tackles this job, everyone involved should have the opportunity to accept the final product. *Shared values are absolutely essential to the success of any group or organization.*

8
The Daycare Center

With every rising of the sun, think of your life as just begun.
—Unknown

It's difficult to assign any one part of the neighborhood campus more importance than the others, but if we could it would
probably be the daycare center. This center, together with the
parents and other role models in the community, has the greatest impact on the life scripts your children will be writing during their earliest years. The daycare center is essential to parents, allowing them the freedom to concentrate on their work
and their parenting education, and it provides an opportunity
for all of the community to share in the development of the
children and participate in the campus.

The Daycare Center: The Ideal Model

Kindergarten is not part of the mandatory education system,
so it is included as part of the design of the daycare center. The
kindergarten teachers in your school and teachers with
degrees in early education will be in charge of the daycare center.

Seniors, parents, singles, and children from the neighborhood spend a scheduled amount of time at the center working with the teachers, assisting on a one-to-one basis or in groups. The schedule allots a certain number of hours each year to each neighborhood resident, depending upon the size of the neighborhood population. For adults who work during the day, those whose work schedules and responsibilities allow for no flexibility, or those with handicaps that make it difficult to meet this obligation have the option of alternative ways to participate. They can spend their allotted hours in some capacity within their limits, either at or for the neighborhood campus, such as reviewing video tapes being considered for use in the schools.

The daycare center is diversified enough to offer people flexibility in meeting their obligations. The hours of operation, set to meet the needs of those who will take advantage of the center, are long enough that those who have inflexible work hours can participate before or after their work schedules.

Those residents who do not wish or refuse to participate in the operation of the daycare center cannot take advantage of the services offered there. A requisite for the parents of children in the daycare program and the elementary school is to be willing to share the responsibility for the children's education with the teachers and professional staff. Obviously, parents who do not wish to participate in the neighborhood campus will want to put their children in another daycare program or school.

Students in grades one through twelve spend a scheduled amount of time working with the teachers in the daycare center as part of their curriculum. They receive class credit for their time, and are responsible for reports to their homeroom teacher and class.

Unwed parents in school and nonworking welfare parents help in the daycare center as part of their parent training program.

The daycare center requires two large rooms. One room is divided into smaller units for infants from six to eighteen months. A teacher, with assistance from adult and student aides (who receive credit for home economics or family living classes), is in charge of no more than four infants. The second room is divided into larger units, depending upon the size of the population of children between eighteen months and six years of age.

Funds for the daycare center come from the regular school budget, with additional funding from the Department of Health and Human Services and private industry. Private industry has the opportunity to sponsor a daycare center at the neighborhood campus by providing yearly funds for the salaries of the teachers and the operation of the center. Employees and executives of sponsoring companies also have an opportunity to volunteer some of their time at the centers.

Welfare recipients with children contribute their time to the daycare operation as well as to other centers, such as the arts and recreation center.

Because good teachers are essential to the success of the daycare center, following are some criteria for evaluating applicants. A good daycare teacher

- loves children and likes to play with them;
- respects and listens to children;
- will kneel down to be level with a child's face, and will look into the child's eyes when talking or listening to him or her;
- has a happy disposition and a positive attitude;
- has empathy and compassion for children;
- knows how to set up a warm, congenial, nonthreatening environment;
- is cooperative and works well with other teachers;
- laughs easily and often;
- keeps a list of four or five children to give special attention to each day;
- knows how to deal with a child's feelings;
- knows how to settle arguments appropriate to the children's age levels.

Practical Suggestions for Implementing the Daycare Center

You may hear discussions in your group about some of the points outlined in the ideal plan for the daycare center. Even the authors had differing opinions in a few cases. That is a good thing. Debate clarifies the issues and allows you to deal with objections. You should not only expect some debate, but also welcome it as a valuable part of developing your own plan. Hearing different points of view also allows you to build some flexibility into your plan. For example, singles and seniors may not wish to participate in the daycare center but want to take advantage of other centers at the neighborhood campus. You might clearly state, then, that residents only support the centers that they use. On the other hand, some people who don't have kids of their own may enjoy the opportunity to work with the children at the daycare center. They may feel that time spent in active support of any of the centers offers them the chance to learn or improve marketable skills. You can word your version of the outline to make it clear that all participation is welcome, while support of the centers on the part of residents is required only for those services they use.

One suggestion that may seem out of the ordinary, considering that we're relating your project to that of an organization, is to celebrate your wins. Setting up a neighborhood campus is no small task, but nowhere is it written (certainly not here) that it can't be fun, too. In addition, celebrating the accomplishment of a goal, such as a grand opening of the daycare center, helps build morale. Bolman and Deal (1984) discussed the importance of the symbolic frame in organizations in *Modern Approaches to Understanding and Managing Organizations.* The symbolic frame includes such things as organizational myths and stories, rituals and ceremonies, and metaphors, humor, and play.

Celebrations are a form of play, and play "permits relaxing

the rules in order to explore alternatives. It encourages experimentation, flexibility, and adaptiveness." Bolman and Deal further said, "Metaphors, humor, and play provide ways for individuals and organizations to escape the tyranny of facts and logic, to view organizations and their own participation in them as if they were something new and different from their appearance, and to find creative alternatives to existing choices." In other words, lighten up now and then, celebrate accomplishments, and play a little. It gives you a fresh start when you return to the business of taking back your neighborhood.

This suggestion is included in this chapter because it might be interesting to have the daycare center be the team that handles your group's celebration planning. Of course, the daycare teachers will have a wealth of ideas for creative play, but so might the kids.

9
The Parent Training Center

⇒╬⇐

Our chief want in life is someone who will make us do what we can.
—Ralph Waldo Emerson

Parents are tough to educate, because they always know everything. Don't you remember how yours were (and maybe still are)? Well, that is until it became clear sometime in junior high that they knew absolutely nothing. Of course, it's always "they" who are that way; we as parents would never claim to be so perfectly right all the time. So, when was the last time you said, "Because I said so," to a child?

Seriously, developing the plan for the parent training center may be a little tougher than some of the others. Rather than set it up for you to be against parent training, let's get to the outline. Then we'll come back to some of the questions and issues.

The Parent Training Center: The Ideal Model

This center is free to all parents, pregnant women, and expectant fathers within the geographical boundaries of the district for the neighborhood public elementary school. Participation in parent training is voluntary for parents who take advantage of the childcare and educational programs at the neighborhood center. The general rules for participatory support of the center are the same as those outlined for the daycare center. And pregnant women are encouraged to attend birthing classes and have monthly physical checkups, available at the neighborhood campus.

As part of their parent training, parents actively participate with the infants and small children in the daycare center, with guidance from teachers from the parent training center.

Working parents are required to spend time at the daycare and parent training centers. Depending upon the arrangements they make with their employers, working parents are assigned a certain amount of time each month. They will spend at least one whole day at the center within a specific time period, coordinated by them, their employers, and the neighborhood campus.

Unemployed mothers and fathers spend a specified number of hours in job training at the neighborhood campus if their child is enrolled in the daycare center. If they have not finished school, they may have their children in daycare at the high school depending on the level of school last completed.

Classes are open-ended, allowing a parent to join a class any week. Classes are offered from eight in the morning until ten at night.

Teachers are classroom teachers from all grade levels, social workers, nutritionists, nurses, psychologists, family counselors, medical doctors from the neighborhood, or university staff. Teachers work on a rotating basis at the campus, as arranged by a salaried center coordinator.

The curriculum is designed, organized, and scheduled by members from each center, a school administrator, representatives from the neighborhood campus board, volunteer parents from the neighborhood, and student representatives from grade levels four to twelve.

The curriculum includes courses in
- household management;
- finances and budgeting;
- shopping;
- time management;
- planning long-range goals;
- problem solving;
- decision making;
- social behavior;
- values;
- physiology and hygiene;
- mental hygiene;
- sharing;
- nurturing;
- shared responsibility;
- family cooperation;
- loving;
- balancing family life with work, school, sports, and leisure; and,
- self-image and identity.

Job skills training is available for all new parents who lack a high school diploma, and for those who have finished high school but are unemployed.

English is taught for new immigrants, as well as an introduction to customs, money, shopping, job-interviewing skills, and other concepts important to American culture.

Practical Suggestions for Implementing the Parent Training Center

Okay, now let's talk. Clearly, this is a bare-bones, generic outline, and probably you will hear some heated debate about some of these points. So let's discuss one of them.

The purpose of having parents participate in parent training if their children are in programs at the neighborhood center is so that the entire family is learning together. It's not unlike one of the most effective ways of treating substance abuse. Therapy for a recovering addict is most effective if it includes the entire family, or at least the spouse or significant other. After all, they all got sick together, so they all need to get well together. Now, not all families are sick; many may not be recovering from anything traumatic or otherwise significant. Even in those cases, however, participating in a complete program that offers family skills training to all family members can only improve the strength of the family. Trading the time to support the campus for the benefits of campus programs is certainly a fair exchange, considering what the services and programs would cost on the free market.

Other points in the outline are fairly self-explanatory, even if they also stir some debate. As long as you keep discussion free and open among participants, your group will arrive at solutions that are workable.

Michael Popkin's *Active Parenting: Teaching Cooperation, Courage, and Responsibility* is an excellent book about parenting, and a source of information you might consider for the parent training center. Used by parents, counselors, teachers, and psychologists as one of the best resources for building responsive, healthy, and fulfilled family relationships, this book offers a solid framework for people to become the best parents they can. Popkin is director of the Active Parenting Program, and is also the author of *Active Parenting: A Video-Based Program* and *So Why Aren't You Perfect Yet?*

People *Are* Taking Back
Their Neighborhoods

A state without the means of some change is without the
means of its conservation.
—*Edmund Burke*

Before we get to the business of setting up a neighborhood campus, let's enjoy some success stories. These stories are plentiful, it seems. They serve as sources of ideas as well as inspiration.

From "Giving Kids Hope" by J. Peder Zane,
Parents, **June, 1996**

A bleak playground in downtown San Francisco resembled a giant parking lot, until Lynne Juarez became involved. Her students at Yerba Buena Children's Center now have a place to build sand castles, grow vegetables, and sit on benches to talk where before there was nothing more than monkey bars and slides. "By the time we're done," Juarez says, "we'll have replaced 20,000 square feet of asphalt with a natural environment that lives and breathes."

Many of the two hundred children at the childcare center Juarez directs come from the most densely populated sections of Chinatown, an area that is all concrete and crowded streets. She noticed during a field trip to a nearby park that many of the kids wouldn't sit on the grass or lean on trees because they thought they were dirty. "Scores of volunteers have donated their time and money to erect Tule Elk Park. In the process of building a park, we've built a community." A landscape architect worked for a fraction of his fee, twenty construction workers volunteered fifteen Saturdays to bulldoze the asphalt, and community members and local businesses helped raise money. Still others donated sweat and elbow grease to plant more than one thousand native plants and vegetables.

"An elderly man came every morning to raise the American flag and every evening to lower it," Juarez said. "He had tears in his eyes when he said it was the first flag that had flown in our neighborhood in decades."

The bleak playground is now an inviting play area with gardens that nourish hummingbirds and butterflies as well as inner-city kids and their neighbors. Juarez sees the children's exuberance as they make new discoveries, and the way they cooperate while tending the garden. "In a world of asphalt and concrete," she said, "the kids and the community now have a little oasis where they can touch a different world and be touched by it."

Also from "Giving Kids Hope" by J. Peder Zane, ### *Parents,* June, 1996

Dolores Ollie has managed to build one of the nation's best schools in one of its poorest neighborhoods. "In scandal-plagued Newark, whose schools sank to such low levels last year that the state of New Jersey took control from the local boards, Harriet Tubman is an island of excellence." Eighty-two percent of students at Harriet Ross Tubman Elementary School, where Ollie is principal, scored above the national average in math, 78 percent above average in language skills, and 70 percent above average in reading on the most recent national examinations.

These are the achievements of students who have been dismissed as a problem population. They are children of the working poor, the homeless, and single mothers on public assistance. Ollie said, "Our success proves that just because you're poor doesn't mean you can't learn. If you give people a chance to excel, they will." She points to dedicated teachers, involved parents, and the ability to raise money as the source of her success at the school. A champion grant applicant, Ollie has secured more than $200,000 from foundations to pay for computers, field trips, and enrichment programs beyond the reach of most inner-city public school students.

"We have no metal detectors, no signs plastered on the walls telling kids what they shouldn't do. They know what we expect, and we don't accept anything less from them."

From "Women Who Make a Difference" by Rob Waters, *Family Circle,* **June 7, 1994**

Doriane Miller, M.D., is the medical director of the Maxine Hall Community Health Center in San Francisco. "We noticed that many women were missing their appointments. When they did show up, they had signs of depression and physical complaints. Instead of just giving them medication, we asked, 'Why is this happening?' And the answer we most often heard was, 'I've recently taken over care for my grandchild, and I don't have time to take care of myself.' "

Concerned about the deteriorating health of these African-American patients, Dr. Miller tried to find services to help. Finding no available resources for grandparents, she and her colleague, registered nurse Sue Trupin, started a support group on their own.

Grandparents Who Care was one of the first support groups for grandparents, but now more than three hundred operate nationwide. Today, the need for such groups has reached every ethnic group. One of the grandparents' biggest problems is financial, since most are poor to begin with, and most states provide less money to relatives raising children than to foster parents. Legislators don't see a need to pay people to care for their own relatives.

Members of the group receive help gaining access to money and services they are entitled to, as well as understanding and emotional support. In addition to the pressures of raising young children again, guilt and anger are common among many of the grandparents—like Lois Kincy, Barbara Coleman, and Doris Wilson. Kincy's four grandchildren, from newborn to nine years old, were left on her front doorstep, literally, when her son and his wife were arrested on drug charges. Coleman's niece, fighting her own battle with drugs, left Coleman with her three children to raise, along with two granddaughters for whom she was already caring. Wilson, who is raising her six-year-old grandson, said, "I felt guilty when some of my kids got on drugs, 'cause I thought maybe I wasn't affectionate enough. But now, I realize it was their choice. Now I'm just gonna try to save my grandson."

Dr. Miller is happy about the organization's growth—there are six groups that meet weekly, led by counselors and specially trained grandparents—but saddened that the problem has required that growth. She is most pleased that the group has succeeded in developing leadership skills among the grandmothers. "I feel as if I've helped people to find their own answers to their problems," she said.

From "Activist Moms" by Michael Orey, *Woman's Day*, August 6, 1996

The article begins with the statement "They were ordinary women, living everyday lives, until some outrage fueled their passion and ignited in them a need to change the system. It could happen to you." Almost five years ago, the need was ignited in Teresa Morris, who didn't even read the newspaper because all that awful news upset her. She did care passionately, however, that her husband and three children were safe and happy.

In early September 1992, a child was reported missing

from her home about five minutes away from the Morris's neighborhood. Teresa and many other local residents helped search for her. "I was so afraid for my own kids during that time," she said. The body of the little girl, molested before she was killed, was found several days later in a plastic garbage bag in a creek.

Morris started thinking of ways to better identify abused children and to prevent further abuse. It was a better plan than focusing her anger on the molester and murderer, the uncle of the little girl. She learned that her state legislator had introduced a measure to expand the definition of abuse in state laws. She convinced the PTA at her local elementary school to approve a resolution supporting the revised child-abuse statute. Besides writing editorials and sending letters to key legislators, Morris worked with her fellow PTA members to implement measures that further protected their children. They had their children fingerprinted at school, found a karate teacher to teach a self-defense course, and introduced an abuse-education program for kids called Good Touch, Bad Touch.

Morris spoke at the state PTA convention in October 1993. The convention gave its unanimous support for the child-abuse legislation, which was passed by the legislature and signed into law by the end of the year.

"I was a very laid-back person," she noted. "I kind of kept to myself. But I've become outspoken and informed. These days, I read the daily paper cover to cover. And I vote."

From "Communities Against Crime" by Marc Kaufman, *Parents*, June 1996

The neighborhood looked so peaceful and friendly, Tony and Laurie Ammirato thought when they moved into the $200,000 Cape Cod-style home. Before long, they learned how very wrong they had been. The four boys across the street fought constantly, vandalized property, lit fireworks in their house. Neighbors and even the parents of the boys frequently called the police. "They just made life in the neighborhood horrible," said Tony, after he had called the police when he thought one of the boys had pulled a real gun on his son.

Ammirato put his house up for sale, but no one wanted to buy it. So, in desperation, he and his neighbors turned to Safe Streets Now! Founded by California mother Molly Wetzel in 1989, Safe Streets Now! programs are operating around the country. The group's tactics include enlisting dozens of neighbors to complain and, if necessary, haul the property owner into court. Ammirato and his neighbors enlisted fifteen families and thirty-four anonymous complainants. Each sued the parents of the wild boys for $5,000. Within weeks of their suit, a California judged ruled in the community's favor, assessing damages of $170,000. Ammirato and his neighbors hope the family will have to sell their home to pay the damages.

Frustrated parents are increasingly turning to this kind of activism. The criminal-justice system and police seem to be unable to deal with the increasing number of drug-related and behavior problems. Betsy Bredau, a Safe Streets Now! coordinator who helped Ammirato organize his suit, said this inability of the system "doesn't mean we're helpless. We can go to small-claims court against the people ruining our blocks, and our experience is that we usually win."

10
The After-School Arts and Recreation Center

To be able to fill leisure intelligently is the last product of civilization.
—Bertrand Russell, The Conquest of Happiness

Every child is an artist. The problem is how to remain an artist
once he grows up. *—Pablo Picasso*

Arts and humanities seem to be falling down on the education system's list of priorities lately. Many of us believe the so-called soft subjects—art, music, literature, philosophy, and so on—are just as important as the hard subjects. True, the effects of an education that includes the humanities are difficult to measure. Unlike science or engineering or business classes, there are not necessarily any jobs automatically associated with humanities except for a few people. How many philosophers do you know personally?

The January 17, 1996, issue of the *Denver Post* carried an article titled "Campus Unruliness Rises" about the rise in disciplinary problems on college campuses that administrators have noticed. Staff writer Mark Eddy wrote that behavior problems more commonly seen in elementary, junior high and high school—rude behavior, inattention, threats and physical intimidation—have increased at universities. Eddy quoted Al Yates, president of Colorado State University, saying, "What we saw years ago in elementary and secondary schools is percolating into institutions of higher education." Society may be paying a price for downgrading the importance of studying the humanities, and emphasizing the importance of technology and adopting a win-at-all-cost attitude. The arts and humanities taught people such qualities as patience, manners, and discipline. They softened the harder edges of humankind. "It makes one ask the question, 'Have we missed somewhere in terms of our definition of education, in our rush to turn out technocrats?' It may well be that in doing so, we may have lost an important piece of our humanity as well. . . . It may be that now we're beginning to see some of the consequences of that in this loss of decorum."

The after-school arts and recreation center offers a chance to supplement regular school classes with some of the humanities. It's not just for kids, either. Adults and seniors also have access to this center.

The After-School Arts and Recreation Center: The Ideal Model

Participation at the arts and recreation center is mandatory for all children from daycare up to and including sixth grade from two to six in the afternoon.

The city's Department of Education and the Department of Parks and Recreation administrate the center.

Physical education teachers, fine arts and crafts teachers, and personnel from the city's Department of Parks and Recreation manage the center.

Administration of salaried employees remains under the jurisdiction of the agency for which they work.

Operations that require student attendance end at 6:00 P.M. All students remain on the school grounds under the supervision of certified teachers until that time. Babies in the daycare center also receive care until 6:00 P.M.

Center operation continues until 11:00 P.M. for adults. Recreational and learning activities are held in the classrooms, gym, multipurpose room, and on the playfields. Activities are planned until 10:00 P.M. for singles, parents, and seniors.

A schedule is available for residents of the neighborhood four times a year.

Chess players, bridge players, and participants in other similar games compete against players from other neighborhoods. Orchestras or other organized groups of this nature may include participants from other neighborhoods.

Evening classes include basic and technical skills such as computer technology, English, drama, chorus, and parent training.

Practical Suggestions for Implementing the After-School Arts and Recreation Center

You may have some adults living in your neighborhood who have expertise in art, music, dance, or any number of other subjects that would be excellent additions to the center curriculum. Many of these people may be willing to share their knowledge with the staff, volunteers, and students. These people can be wonderful gifts to your program. You might want to draft an orientation for these potential part-time teachers so they meld into the curriculum and are consistent with your teaching standards. As usual, salaries for these teachers should be appropriate for their teaching experience and degree of proficiency in their fields.

"Are Kids' Sports Safe," an article by Martha Raddatz in the June/July 1996 issue of *Child* magazine, offered some good news about children and organized sports. "Research has long shown that boys develop important skills from competitive sports, including an ability to work with a team, to perform under pressure, to set goals, and to accept criticism. The news is even more encouraging for girls," Raddatz continued. "A study by the Women's Sports Foundation in East Meadow, New York, revealed that girls involved in sports are less likely to use drugs or get pregnant and more likely to graduate from high school."

The same article included five tips for good sports parenting.

- Kids should have fun playing sports, and that should always be the most important reason for them to play. Put their interests first.
- Your time, and any other assistance you can offer, can help your child have a successful experience with sports.
- Sports programs that are consistent with the values and philosophy you would like your child to learn are always wise choices.
- Be supportive, but do so quietly from the sidelines. Let the coach teach and work with your child.
- Clarify the goals you want your child to be aiming to achieve—for example, trying hard, enjoying him- or herself, and improving skills.

Finally, Raddatz said the American Academy of Pediatrics in Chicago recommends waiting until children are six years old before letting them play competitive sports. Before that age, they do best in unstructured environments that allow them to experiment with different skills.

A child's mind and body atrophy without constant nurturing and attention. Herbert Kohl (1978) maintained that "intellectual, emotional and physical strength are components of mind in its broadest definition." These elements enable a child to grow into a centered, whole person. Encouraging children's development of these strengths also provides them with options for releasing stress, anger, and frustration in positive ways as they grow into adulthood. As personal strength grows, so does self-respect. Kohl suggested, "this authentic sense of personal growth and power, which constitutes self-respect, underlies the development of caring and strong children. Without self-respect, it is not possible to continue learning, growing, and forming good character."

11
The Health and Human Services Center

Look to your health; and if you have it, praise God, and value it next to a good conscience; for health is the second blessing that we mortals are capable of; a blessing that money cannot buy. —Izaak Walton

It's odd to think that Izaak Walton died in 1683, before people could even dream of the medical technology we have today. Odd because health probably was considered a gift of God or pure luck during that time, and therefore could not be bought.

Unfortunately, there is some room for debate these days about whether money can buy health. Everybody seems to be upset about healthcare for one reason or another, and one of those reasons is the cost. However, there is a piece of information that points to the possibility that indeed money can buy health.

The neighborhood health and human services center offers the opportunity to equalize access to a number of health services. Ian Robertson (1987) wrote:

> Your chances of enjoying good health are improved if two conditions are met: first, that your living conditions tend not to induce disease; and second, that you have access to

good healthcare. People with these advantages will tend to have consistently better health than those who lack them: in other words, there will be inequality of health in the society. Differences in health status, like other forms of social inequality, tend to be based on differences in socio-economic status. . . . There is a consistent relationship between social status and health status, with lower-income people having higher rates of most diseases and mental disorders, and therefore, shorter life expectancies. In the United States, as everywhere else, social and economic background literally affect one's life chances.

More healthcare plans seem to attempt to reward preventative practices, rather than offer benefits only after illness or disease has already set in. The health and human services center offers health services regardless of income and will provide many of those services necessary to prevent illness or detect early signs of disease.

The Health and Human Services Center: The Ideal Model

The health and human services center offers a series of immunization shots during the child's first year.

The center maintains records for each child, including information on physical checkups, vaccinations, shots, allergies (environmental, food, contact, and prescription drug), vision, and hearing.

Nurse practitioners and dental hygienists visit the campus periodically to detect diseases and prevent them from spreading.

Nurses conduct classes with students, parents, seniors, and teachers on topics relating to physical and mental health, disease symptoms and control, and social sexual behavior and protection.

Nurses are available to perform weekly checkups for

seniors, including blood pressure, pulse, and weight checks, prescription drug medication monitors, and nutrition evaluations.

Social workers, psychologists, and mental health workers are available depending on the population and needs of the neighborhood. These professionals consult with students, families, and teachers.

Center staff will visit the home of each child at least once a year.

Prenatal and postnatal care is provided for every expectant mother in the neighborhood. A licensed practical nurse, licensed midwife, or medical doctor administers this care.

Practical Suggestions for Implementing the Health and Human Services Center

An endless list of classes, workshops, and seminars exists for possible inclusion in your health and human services center. Registered dietitians can discuss topics ranging from proper nutritional management of gestational diabetes to safe weight loss to a rotation diet for food allergies. A chef or cook could discuss proper food handling and storage, two very important factors in the prevention of illness. Knowledgeable mental health professionals could talk about some of the interesting studies of the effect of thought on illness and disease.

This center is a great choice for contests like "best low fat, low calorie" dishes, "best vegetarian" dishes, and "best healthy desserts," to name just a few. Taste tests would fit in quite well with a neighborhood potluck dinner.

Hospitals are often sources of endless interesting pieces of information as well as programs they will offer to community residents. Practitioners of various therapies, both mental and physical, are another possibility for interesting alternatives in the area of holistic health. Massage therapy is one example of this type of program.

There seems to be an overwhelming abundance of information about all kinds of regimens, vitamins, disciplines, and practices that claim to make us younger, keep us healthier, cure life-threatening diseases, and slim us down. What's even more confusing is that much of this information is supposed to be based on legitimate studies. Even worse is that those studies often contradict each other. One really good idea for the entire community is a seminar or workshop series—perhaps quarterly—that reviews the pros and cons of different products and how to make informed decisions about whether to try them. Drug and food interactions is another possible topic, especially concerning over-the-counter drugs that most people assume to be safe.

Finally, many people believe there is a spiritual element to health. Deepak Chopra (1994) wrote, "Health is not just the absence of a disease. It's an inner joyfulness that should be ours all the time—a state of positive well-being." Your health and human services center might consider programs on such topics for those who are interested.

12
The Senior Center

≈╪╪≈

Every man desires to live long; but no man would be old.
—Jonathan Swift

In earlier chapters we discussed the baby boomers and generation X, and we talked some about seniors in chapter 2. Seniors, too, have a generational name, although it is less familiar. They are the New Elders.

The boomers are sweeping into middle age and appear to have every intention, as a group, of changing the face of aging. However, most of the time when we think in stereotypical images of "old" people, we aren't thinking about those born between the mid-teens and the mid-thirties—the New Elders. We're probably actually picturing their parents, those who are over seventy-five right now. Why? Because the baby boomers have role models for a different way of aging—their parents. This age group is "the first older generation to arrive at their later years with a majority still relatively healthy, active, and affluent. They are the New Elders, who have aged in a time when becoming old is so different from what people their age experienced in the past that they have been forced to undertake the reinvention of old age" (Gerber et al. 1989, 2).

People are living longer, so when we look at the senior center ideal model we have to keep in mind that we are considering at least two distinctly different generations. The New Elders are decidedly different from their parents' generation, and their activities may be different. In addition, "some contemporary grandparents are opting for distance instead of closeness, choosing to attend to their own busy lives and let their children raise their grandchildren. They are forsaking anything resembling the traditional role of grandparent" (Gerber et al. 1989, 25). So the senior citizens in your neighborhood may not all be interested in becoming surrogate grandparents for the neighborhood.

The Senior Center: The Ideal Model

Use of the learning center, or school, for children ends at 2:00 P.M. After that time, the classrooms are available for the after-school arts and recreation center and the senior center.

Seniors participate in planned activities or use the classrooms for socializing or adult education classes.

Seniors, parents, volunteers, and members of the neighborhood participate in all school activities planned for children, such as potluck meals. They are welcome to join the audience for videos, plays, musicals, lectures, and sports events.

Seniors who are willing can demonstrate crafts to, offer entertainment to, or share job experiences with students and the rest of the neighborhood.

Seniors as well as students of all ages visit home-bound residents or convalescent homes as a group. A coordinator arranges the joint participation, which also includes taking babies to the homes for the elderly to enjoy and hold if it is appropriate.

Meals are available for seniors every day if they wish to have them. Seniors join other neighborhood residents in assisting nutritionists and cooks in meal planning, serving, and cleaning up.

Meals are scheduled with the children so that seniors and children can enjoy a family-type atmosphere.

Practical Suggestions for Implementing the Senior Center

Seniors have an opportunity at the campus to be around people of different ages. They can offer their experience and wisdom to help children learn about life and the meaning of family. They might enjoy having some involvement in managing the neighborhood campus. They might also, however, enjoy just having a place close to their homes that offers hot meals, free healthcare, classes, and a place to socialize with their peers and other age groups.

Another group to consider is that of New Elders who may be raising their grandchildren, for whatever reason. Parenting classes and other activities planned for the parents can include these community members as well. Grandparents who have the chance to have their grandchildren visit for a period of time could also participate in the family activities and programs. This group of visiting children could be very important to spreading the idea of the neighborhood campus to other communities, when they take their experiences at the campus back home with them.

13
The Twenty-Four Hour
Crisis Center

*The golden rule is, to help those we love to escape from us; and never try to begin
to help people, or influence them till they ask, but wait for them.*
—Friedrich von Hugel

The format of this chapter is somewhat different from chapters
about the other neighborhood campus centers. The ideal
model really only has two items. The hours of operation are
already defined. The twenty-four-hour crisis center is also different because it has essentially one purpose: to provide a safe
place for people in the neighborhood to turn to if they are in
danger or in crisis.

You should design the crisis center with qualified therapists
or social workers. The neighborhood residents who will be
operating the center should have some training in crisis management and intervention, but their primary role is not to
resolve the problem but to remove the person from the situation. The staff, which should include at least one licensed
counselor during all hours of operation, should be prepared to
keep victims safe and to locate a safe place for them to stay as
soon as possible. The licensed counselor will see that the trou-

bled person has appropriate counseling and support.

The counseling community is aware that building family strength is critical to the webbing that holds neighborhoods together. Cynthia Moreno (*Counselor* 1996, January/ February) wrote a column about vision and commitment to communities from the counselor's viewpoint. Her title for the piece was, appropriately, "Communities: The Vital Link." That mission, she reported, should be to reduce mental illness and substance abuse in the population with which counselors work, and to reduce the harms associated with those disorders. That mission shifts the counselor's practice from individuals to communities and from treatment only to prevention and intervention. Their practices need to expand to include more of the communities in which their clients and families live. "We are not talking about 'harm reduction' here," Moreno continued, "but about providing a full continuum of services and care." One of the ways counselors can do that, she said, is to join a community group or coalition. "We can infiltrate community systems with our knowledge, experience and hope."

Mental health counselors and many other health professionals do see the need for intervention at the family and community level, and may quite willingly offer their professional services to your neighborhood campus.

So the first step is to provide a safe place to which children, teens, and adults can come when they are in danger, supervised by licensed practitioners. The second step is to ensure that your network of follow-up support services and staff is in place to offer these people the means to stay out of harm's way. And third, part of those services should include family therapy and counseling.

When we talked about generation X in earlier chapters, we promised to present the other side of their list of characteristics. Some of these young people may be well suited to working in the crisis center. As a group, they are not lacking in ambition or promise. In fact, again as a group, they are better educated than any generation raised in this country. And "they have demonstrated a passion for social and environmental issues. More of them are choosing science and service careers than ever before, and community volunteerism is at an all-time high" (*Counselor* 1995, January/February). As usual, not all of the generation Xers are alike and not all of them fit the typical profile. They bring their own background, unique to their generation, to the party.

One last idea is to take the crisis center to the streets, so to speak. Many neighborhoods, as we've discussed, have set up neighborhood patrols. These patrollers may come across victims trying to get away, or who can't escape the abuser. In the *Denver Post*, July 18, 1996, in an article entitled "Neighborhood Patrols to Get Free Cell Phones," Robert A. Rankin reported that initially, about 50,000 cell phones will be donated to citizen-patrol groups as part of the Communities on Phone Patrol (COPP) program. The donor trade group, Cellular Telecommunications Industry Association, offered the grant and free air time so the phones can work. The donation costs the taxpayers nothing.

Rankin ended by saying neighborhood groups seeking phones should contact local police, or COPP in Washington, D.C.

There is plenty of help for your project out there. People are just waiting for you to ask.

Conclusion

My observation that a profound transformation of consciousness is taking place in our world at this time is based on the changes I see within myself, those around me, and in our society. It is affirmed by feedback I receive from thousands of people I work with all over the world.
—Shakti Gawain, Living in the Light

When we think of a village model, we may actually be thinking of a model village. We think that when people lived in villages, society seemed more stable. Everybody knew each other, so there was less crime. People understood the rules and suffered less anxiety and little confusion about their identities. The principle of shared responsibility worked because survival depended upon it. The village, like an extended family, nurtured the children.

This picture may be somewhat idealistic. It doesn't include the sweat and the frustration that the villagers must have felt at times. Knowing that some of the villagers probably had gnarly warts doesn't really matter. What we see in our minds is the scene with Harrison Ford and Alexander Godunov building that barn in *Witness*, while Kelly McGillis smiled mysteriously as she poured cold lemonade for them.

The truth about how it really was back in the village days doesn't matter. What matters and what we can build upon is the part of the image that inspires us. We will never go back in time to see if our picture is accurate. But we don't care; we have what we need from the past.

In our pursuit of technology, we lost the village. Along the way we lost our values and the relative simplicity of a value-driven life. Yet this isn't quite accurate, either. We can't have completely lost our values, or we wouldn't miss them. That vision of the village is still with us, even if tangled up in the power cords of all this technology.

Perhaps, then, there is hope that we're not lost. Maybe what has happened is we've forgotten what made values important while we've dealt with all our everyday worries. This part requires more thought, because the truth about the present does matter, for the present is where we can change things, but only if we really know what we're changing.

So in anticipating change, we return again to an ideal, a model. We must see ourselves recovering our identities. We can imagine ourselves as heroes.

A vision draws the best from the past, includes the truth of the present, and predicts an ideal future. The value of a powerful vision, however, doesn't live in whether or not it is ever realized exactly like the picture; the value comes from the questions: What will it take for us to live as if we can do this? and Who do we have to become to get there from here?

John Heider (1986) wrote:

Any overdetermined behavior produces its opposite:
An obsession with living suggests worry about dying.
True simplicity is not easy.
Is it a long time or a short time since we last met?
The braggart probably feels small and insecure.
Who would be first ends up last.

Knowing how polarities work, the wise leader does not push to make things happen, but allows process to unfold on its own.

144

The leader teaches by example rather than by lecturing others on how they ought to be.

The leader knows that constant interventions will block the group's process. The leader does not insist that things come out a certain way.

Ironically, you have to create the vision, only to give up insisting that it be achieved. You lead effectively by allowing others the freedom to become leaders. And your own answer to the question Who do I have to become to make this happen? is, a leader.

Before you can even worry about that, the next question pops up: How do we get there from here? You write down an answer, and ask the question again. And again and again, until you have a plan. Then you and your neighbors do those things, and before long you have a barn. Perhaps not exactly like the one in the movie, but it's a barn and it works.

So there you are. Your barn, right in the middle of your village.

Appendix A:
Establishing Your
Neighborhood Campus

＝＋＋＝

Organize Your Study Group

You'll save yourself a great deal of pain and work if you organize a core group of neighbors who are interested in the neighborhood campus. Start talking with your neighbors. See who becomes excited about the campus concept.

Meet Your Neighbors

Make a list of the families with children enrolled in your neighborhood elementary school. Telephone the parents or send them a form letter inviting them to your home for the first organizational meeting.

Form a committee to find out how many seniors, singles, and married couples live in the neighborhood.

Use your local newspaper to spread the news about your project. Write letters to the editor inviting neighbors to join your group. Have someone write press releases or articles about your neighborhood campus. Set up committees to divide the time and energy required from team members.

Choose the most enthusiastic people and invite them to be on the planning committee. Try to put together a group that reflects the composition of the neighborhood. For example, if singles and seniors live in the neighborhood, see if some of them will be part of the planning committee. Include representatives for each of the different family structures (two-parent, single-parent, and so on). Representatives of each of the different paid staff positions should also be included, from school administrators and teachers to counselors and medical personnel.

Know Your Elementary School

Become involved with the elementary school in your neighborhood. If you don't have time during the day, attend meetings and events at the school in the evenings, even if you don't have children enrolled there. Get to know the administrators and staff.

If you are working full time, try to find at least an hour during the day once a month that you can spend at the school.

Spark your employer's interest. Describe the benefits of the campus from an employer's viewpoint—better attendance and increased productivity, in particular. Prepare presentations to companies, complete with actual and estimated figures. Industry is a potential source of financing. Many companies support community projects to increase good will.

Study the Physical Assets of the School and School Grounds

Make a list of the number of rooms in the school. Note the sizes and numbers of rooms, and any special functions they may serve (lunchroom, library, gymnasium, and so on). Make a list of the number of rooms you need for the neighborhood campus and for what purpose.

Study Charter Schools

If possible, go visit a charter school. Write to some charter schools and ask for their advice for starting one.

Form a committee to study the financial and legal design of a charter school.

Find out what funds are available for charter schools.

Consider how you can apply the rules for charter schools to your neighborhood campus.

Know Your Subject

Taking back your neighborhood is a very complex project. The neighborhood campus involves many concepts and drastic changes. Be prepared for all the arguments for and against.

Know your statistics and study your sources. You will find data in one book to be entirely different from data in another.

Someone once said, "If you can't explain an idea in one sentence, you'll lose your audience."

Be prepared for a long battle, but don't let yourself burn out. You can avoid burnout by delegating assignments and keeping enough people involved. Rotate leaders regularly. Initiate the practice of having the groups remind each other to remember balance.

Study the Sample Curriculum Based on Ecology

Form a team to study the curriculum.

Inquire at a nearby university if any professors would be interested in being involved by sharing their expertise in ecology, integrated subjects, and interdisciplinary studies.

Involve educators who specialize in outdoor education and conservation, as well as leaders in active outdoor groups such as the Audubon Society, Wildlife Society, and the Nature Conservancy.

Investigate the availability of funds from foundations to hire a full-time curriculum director. The curriculum director would prepare a curriculum for daycare through sixth grade.

Have one group remain active after you've launched the neighborhood campus. This group will monitor the campus for at least five years to see if it is successful. Since the campus is a new concept, the group will recommend changes and adjustments to the plan. Keep your goals and objectives clear, polish your sense of humor, and enjoy the pride in your community.

You can make your community work.

Appendix B:
A Sample Curriculum Based on Ecology

Every living thing potentially affects every other living thing and the physical environment of the planet. —Paul and Anne Erlich, Extinction

We are not born to be what we are. We are given hope or taught fear. We live in a time of progress or we live amid a century's moment of chaos. And finally, we send our children to a school system full of experiments and inquiries or to one that is set in its ways and unwilling to budge much for anyone.
—Robert Coles, Children in Crisis

People have a few problems these days. People in the United States are facing an educational crisis, for example. Education in the US ranks the lowest of all industrialized western countries in academic achievement, the amount of time spent in classrooms, participation in sports, and in the health of our children. Over 20 million adults lack the basic skills needed in today's job market. According to "The Literary Gap," an article in the December 19, 1988, *Time*, this "skills deficit has cost businesses and taxpayers $20 billion in lost wages, profits, and productivity. Remedial training costs industry $300 million a year. . . . Two-thirds of employees in remedial classes are high school graduates. One out of four high school graduates has the equivalent of an eighth-grade education." In California, 50 percent of newly admitted college students are in remedial classes that cost the state $127 million.

People of the world face a global ecological crisis. We know about the destruction of the rainforests and how that has affected the world. In the US, in what was once named The Great Desert on maps, farmers found the largest plain of the richest soil in the world. They tilled large acres of land, over-turning the soil, preparing to plant their crops. And during the great drought in the 1920s and 1930s, farmers, ignorant of the effect of wind on loose soil on a large flat plain, watched their land disappear in terrible dust storms.

In contrast, east of the Cascade Mountains in Washington State dams along the Columbia River turned the arid land into a vibrant green landscape. Orchards hug the sides of the river, and wheat, grape vines, barley, and hops fill the valleys and wide flat plains. The dams provide the Pacific Northwest with an abundance of cheap hydroelectric power. The area is a mar-velous example of people's ability to live in partnership with the environment.

Jane Goodall (1990), who has spent thirty years studying chimpanzees in Gombe on the shores of Lake Tanganyika, wrote:

Today, striding the face of the globe, humans clear the trees, lay waste the land, cover mile after mile of rich earth with concrete. Humans tame the wilderness and plunder its riches. We believe ourselves all powerful. But it is not so.

Relentlessly the desert inches forward, gradually replacing the life-sustaining trees with barren and uncom-promising harshness. Plant and animal species vanish, lost to the world before we have learned of their value, their place in the great scheme of things. World temperatures soar, the ozone layer is depleted. All around we see destruc-tion and pollution, war and misery, maimed bodies and dis-torted minds, human and non-human alike.

If we allow this desecration to continue, we shall, our-selves, be doomed. We cannot meddle so greatly in the master plan and hope to survive. Thinking of this whole terrible picture, the magnitude of our sins against nature, against our fellow creatures, I was overwhelmed. How could I—or anyone—make a difference in the face of such vast and mindless destruction.

Each of us can make a difference if we work with our neighbors to practice shared responsibility for the quality of our children's education and development of their respect for ecology. We can offer ourselves as models of stewardship so that when our children become the administrators, engineers, and city planners, they will have the tools to preserve our planet.

John H. Storer (1968) said: "Hungry people crowd into cities, concentrating frustration, despair and alienation in tightly packed explosive mixtures. The key to success [is] the search for a clearer understanding of the forces that shape human motivation. The need now is for human wisdom to build an environment where men and women can develop and carry forward the motivations for civilized living."

One way we can build such an environment is to study a curriculum in ecology.

Ecology is the study of the interdependence and interrelationship of organisms and their environments. The whole system of organisms in their dependence on each other and on features of the nonliving environment makes up an ecosystem. The ecosystem consists of populations of organisms living together in communities in a particular habitat such as the desert or the ocean. There are four fundamental cycles that affect the ecosystem: the water cycle; the oxygen and carbon dioxide cycle and photosynthesis; the nitrogen cycle; and the food chain cycle—the producers, consumers, and decomposers. Ecosystems have been called "the delicate balance of nature," because if one organism or any nonliving matter in an ecosystem is disturbed, all other members of that community become distressed.

In a human ecosystem, the nature of a family's interactions with each other and with their community tells you about the health and happiness of both.

John H. Storer (1968) quotes Dr. Robert M. MacIver: "In every community there is a force, or authority, that is greater than the authority of government; this is the consensus of the community opinion." Storer continues, "The success of human society in another year, or ten years, will depend in large measure on the foundation that is being laid in today's environment. The foundation is built by the quality of minds that its education turns out, the quality of the opportunity that it offers to these minds, and the quality of the motivation that its houses and traditions instill in those minds."

A curriculum based on ecology offers a set of values that fosters stewardship for this planet, a direct responsibility for nurturing the earth's health. Such a curriculum reminds us that man is not superior here, but is interdependent with all other animals and plants.

If this planet is to survive with a healthy atmosphere for plants and animals, man must stop using carbon fuels. Consider the possibilities of a world agreement among all nations that would suggest the following steps:

- formation of an international group of scientists and industrial leaders to find a practical application for solar power and nuclear fusion that will not pollute our environment;
- continuing space programs and research as an international endeavor;
- rationing of petroleum products worldwide;
- preservation of all wilderness areas, watersheds, wild game habitats, and old timber and rain forests;
- development of an ecologically sound plan for reestablishing healthy soil through proper planting, for land that has been misused and depleted or eroded away causing flood plains to be silted;
- abolishment of chemical fertilizers, and education in

organic and ecological methods for controlling pests and adding nutrients;
• preservation of all mammals in our oceans, and of all wetlands;
• abolishment of fishing methods such as dragnetting, and adoption of stricter fishing limits to safeguard future supplies of fish;
• protection of all watersheds and streams from contamination from cattle-feeding lots and from the clear cutting of timber, especially near salmon migrating streams;
• institution of annual inspections of septic tank and drain field systems within a certain distance of bodies of water, to protect bivalve shellfish from contamination;
• rationing of drinking water and hydroelectric power worldwide;
• prohibiting use of water for ornamental plantings not native to a habitat and establishing programs to foster cultivation of native plants;
• changing patterns of misusing the environment and establishing programs to cultivate crops, fish, and minerals ecologically suitable to a geographic area;
• balancing economic rewards for residents of these areas by teaching innovative skills for working and trading in harmony with the environment;
• decentralizing metropolitan areas worldwide to lessen the burden on public utilities, transportation, the environment, and inhabitants, and to provide a more aesthetic, higher quality of life;
• limiting the size of cities and their environs to protect and safeguard a sufficient water supply and to control the level of underground water tables.

The following is an example of how a curriculum based on ecology would operate. This is only a partial curriculum, focusing on just one of the four fundamental cycles of an ecosystem: the water cycle.

How to Protect Our Water: A Project

The following projects involve members of the whole family. They begin at home, involving children in conservation education, and culminate in building an exhibit to show at the local fair. It may be necessary at times to consult with a professional ecologist, or even a science teacher at your local high school to get help in understanding these topics yourself. These projects are suggested merely as an outline to follow on your own path of study. First, however, we must understand the types of waste and erosion we're dealing with.

I. Types of wastes
   A. Human wastes: sewer treatment plants and septic tanks
   B. Wastewater from flooding and storm drainage systems
   C. Animal wastes from farmlands and stock feeding stations, and runoff of polluted water and nitrogen into waterways
   D. Sea mammal wastes from highly concentrated colonies of sea lions at the mouths of rivers into tidelands; effects of this waste material on shellfish beds
   E. Wastewater polluted with oils from large tarred parking lots
   F. Hazardous wastes; use of environmentally sound and biodegradable pest controls, garden fertilizers, cleaning and painting products

II. Erosion: controlling surface runoff and erosion
   A. Effects of erosion on salmon migration
   B. Effects of erosion on water, land, habitats, ecosystems, and agriculture

Sewer Systems Project

Make an illustrated exhibit of a sewer system and a sewer treatment center.

- Illustrate how toxic chemicals affect fish in our waterways.
- Show a septic system and how it works. Include its proper use and problems, and how to monitor it. What pathogens are and how they effect humans, animals, and fish.
- Illustrate a storm sewer drainage system and how it controls fuels and oil wastes from automobiles. Illustrate how it controls mud slides to keep them from destroying homes and highways.
- Illustrate a stock feed station and how to keep the wastes and high concentrations of nitrogen from getting into our waterways.

Wetland and Watershed Project

I. What is a watershed and how do wastes affect it? Why is it important?
II. What is a wetland and why is it important to humans as well as our earth? Illustrate a watershed showing the effects on our land and in our waterways.

How to involve children from four years to third grade

I. Start in the home. Help them answer the following questions:
- Where does the water in your home come from?
- Where does the water go from your laundry, garbage disposal, sinks, bathtubs, and toilets?
- Where does rainwater run off from the roof of your home and garage and paved driveway?

- What methods have you used to stop erosion from roof runoffs?
- What is bacteria and why do we need toilets, sewers, and septic tanks?

II. Find ways to conserve water around your house.

III. Look around your school and discuss storm sewer drainage with older students. Locate drains around the school. Look for erosion from rain drainage with older students. Is the topography such that there are wet or damp spots on the school grounds? How can this be fixed? How can you help conserve water in your classroom and bathrooms? How can you help keep your schools clean to reduce causes of diseases?

IV. Younger children can help the older children keep the school buildings and grounds clear of trash. Designate an area in a covered part of the school to collect all the trash gathered in one week to show how much trash people make. How can we eliminate trash from our environment? What can manufacturers do to eliminate trash?

A. Illustrate a storm sewer site.

B. Write a story about conserving water or keeping yourself and your school clean.

C. Illustrate what bacteria or pathogens found in sewers look like under a microscope.

Projects for older students

I. Using the same questions as above, go into more detail with illustrations, exhibits, dioramas, and hands-on exhibits to show how erosion happens without proper storm drain sewers in your community.

II. Involve the younger children in discussions and trips to sewer treatment centers, to areas where erosion has caused damage to the environment, and to farmlands that have proper control of water runoff.

III. Build a model of a primary, secondary, and tertiary treatment plant.

At the Fair: An Exhibit

When you've completed the previous projects, you'll be ready to take it to the people, to help educate those in your neighborhood, and even those in other neighborhoods, about protecting our ecosystem. Local fairs are an excellent place to do so. By example, students and families will show the neighborhood how to recycle; if possible, have a recycling center managed by volunteers in their neighborhood. Set up a recycling center at the school. Show the administrators of the neighborhood campus ways to conserve water and to reduce waste and pollution. Show them how to clean the school without using cleansing materials that pollute our water, and air and soil.

Your fair presentation should include the following elements.

- exhibits;
- dioramas;
- illustrations;
- scale models;
- hands-on exhibits to involve those attending the fair;
- plays, songs, and dances about water conservation and protection;
- seminars with audience participation.

An excellent way to get neighbors involved in your fair exhibit is to offer recognition, or even a prize, to the student project group that contributed the most hours and the greatest skill in demonstrating the best ways to solve the problems presented by the project. Likewise, recognition could be offered to the family that had the most outstanding participation on the project.

Appendix C:
The Change Agent Role

Accepting a challenge to change something like a neighborhood is no small undertaking. Change of any degree at all can be frightening to people. At the moment you accept the challenge of change, whether personal or on a grand scale, the identity you've had ends. You begin at that precise moment to become a different person. You have to, because change implies something different from what you've known before, and the new circumstances draw qualities out of you that perhaps you haven't had to use before. Some of those qualities you may not have even known you had.

At that fleeting moment, change looks like death to your identity. It does not want to die, so it tells you to stop what you're doing. However, by then it is too late—you are already different.

Imagine what happens when several people go through this identity death at the same time. That will happen when you start organizing your teams to create the neighborhood center.

The change agent is a leader as well as a facilitator. Max De Pree (1989) said, "The first responsibility of a leader is to define reality. The last is to say thank you. In between the two, the leader must become a servant and a debtor. That sums up the progress of an artful leader."

A change agent is an empowered person, usually empowered by a group, to guide and observe the change process. Often when organizations need to change, they will bring an agent from outside, specifically so he or she can be objective about the process. That's part of the job, to dispassionately evaluate the progress toward the desired goal. The change agent doesn't really think in terms of good or bad, but rather in terms of does it work or not.

The change agent-leader must also become self-empowering, however. He or she doesn't wait for support of a group to begin the change process. The change agent-leader is the one who holds the vision for the project. He or she is the source of empowerment for others on the team or teams precisely because of that vision. It is the change agent-leader who is able to bring it back into sharp focus when people start to forget why they're doing all that hard work.

Almost every model of the change process puts vision at the top; if not at the top, at the beginning of the change cycle. Stephen Covey (1991) said, "Without the same set of criteria, frame of reference, and overall vision, people become adversarial, with a great deal of fighting, rivalry, and polarization breaking down the culture." You want to know that everybody is working on the same project. One thing that doesn't work is if you are clearly envisioning a neighborhood campus, but one of the team members is equally certain you're building a jungle gym and another thinks it's a garage.

Obviously, then, communicating the vision is important. One of the best ways to do that is to create a mission statement with as many people as possible who will be part of the project. The mission statement outlines what you're doing, but more importantly, it says why you're doing it. It is a statement of the values you agree upon as a group for the project. Those values usually would appear on the personal lists of the individuals in the group as well.

Stephen Covey (1994) again has one of the clearest outlines of a mission statement. He says an empowering mission statement

- represents the deepest and best within you;
- is the fulfillment of your own unique gifts (or those of your team);
- is transcendent, meaning it's based on principles of contribution and purpose higher than self;
- addresses and integrates fundamental human needs and capacities: physical, social, mental, and spiritual;
- is based on principles that produce quality-of-life results;
- deals with both vision and principle-based values;
- deals with all the significant roles in your life (or in the life of the team as a unit);
- is written to inspire you, not to impress anyone else.

Probably the single most important thing you can do first is to write your mission statement. There is no right or wrong way for it to sound or look; whatever works for the group is the right format.

❊

The change process itself is actually fairly simple, although people like to make it seem more difficult for some reason. There are two very good, very simple models that differ primarily in the amount of detail—one has some and the other has almost none.

The first is from *The Action Research Planner*. The diagram looks like a spiral, and the description of the process follows.

- to develop a plan of critically informed action to improve what is already happening,
- to act to implement the plan,
- to observe the effects of the critically informed action in the context in which it occurs, and
- to reflect on these effects as a basis for further plan-

ning, subsequent critically informed action and so on, through a succession of cycles.

To do action research is to plan, act, observe and reflect more carefully, more systematically, and more rigorously than one usually does in everyday life; and to use the relationships between these moments in the process as a source of both improvement and knowledge (Kemmis and McTaggart 1988).

The second model, from *Teaching the Elephant to Dance*, looks like a diamond. It contains the following information, starting with Vision at the top.

Vision: Actions, Expectation systems, People systems, and Culture systems
Create Tomorrow: Strategies, Resources
Preparation: Getting ready, Anticipating obstacles
Change: Individual, Organization

That's not all that complicated. It's what you would do anyway, but seeing it helps clarify what you're up to even more.

There is a great deal of discussion around the change process—book after book attempt it in detail. They are helpful to some degree, but the chitchat about change doesn't come anywhere close to describing what the actual process is about. So we're recommending some excellent resources that you can use when and as you need them. This list is in no particular order, and some of these are also contained in the references.

Teaching the Elephant to Dance, by James A. Belasco, Ph.D.
Leadership Is an Art, by Max De Pree
First Things First, by Stephen R. Covey
The Action Research Planner, (Third Edition) by Stephen Kemmis and Robin McTaggart
Enlightened Leadership, by Ed Oakley and Doug Krug
Leaders, by Warren Bennis and Burt Nanus

164

A Manual for Group Facilitators, produced by Center for Conflict Resolution

How to Run a Successful Meeting in Half the Time, by Milo O. Frank

Creative Visualization, by Shakti Gawain

Living in the Light, by Shakti Gawain

It Takes a Village, by Hillary Rodham Clinton

The Transformational Leader, by Noel M. Tichy and Mary Anne Devanna

The Empowered Manager, by Peter Block

Servant Leadership, by Robert K. Greenleaf

The Seven Habits of Highly Effective People, by Stephen R. Covey

Leader Effectiveness Training, by Dr. Thomas Gordon

The Team Handbook, by Peter R. Scholtes and other contributors

Principle-Centered Leadership, by Stephen R. Covey

References

Aburdene, Patricia, and John Naisbitt. 1992. *Megatrends for Women*. New York: Fawcett Columbine.

Adler, Mortimer J. 1982. *The Paideia Proposal*. New York: Macmillan Publishing Co.

___. 1981. *Six Great Ideas*. New York: Macmillan Publishing Co.

Aral, S., and K.K. Holmes. 1991. *Sexually Transmitted Diseases in the AIDS Era*. Scientific American (February).

Auletta, Ken. 1982. *The Underclass*. New York: McGraw-Hill.

Bach, Richard. 1977. *Illusions*. N.p.: Delacorte Press.

Barraclough, Geoffrey, ed. 1984. *The Times Atlas of World History*. Rev. ed. Maplewood, N.J.: Hammond.

Bear Heart, with Molly Larkin. 1996. *The Wind Is My Mother*. New York: Clarkson N. Potter, Inc.

Belasco, James A. 1990. *Teaching the Elephant to Dance*. New York: Crown Publishers.

Berg, Steve. 1993. "Valuing Families." *Star Tribune* (June 6). Minneapolis.

Berman, Morris. 1981. *The Reenchantment of the World*. Ithaca: Cornell University Press.

Bernikow, Louise. 1986. *Alone in America*. New York: Harper & Row.

Billington, Ken. 1988. *People, Politics, and Public Power*. Seattle: Washington Public Utility Districts' Association.

Bolman, Lee G., and Terrence E. Deal. 1984. *Modern*

Approaches to Understanding and Managing Organizations. San
Francisco: Jossey-Bass Inc.

Bowen, Catherine Drinker. 1986. *Miracle at Philadelphia.*
Boston: Little, Brown & Co.

Bronowski, Jacob. 1978. *The Origins of Knowledge and
Imagination.* New Haven, Conn.: Yale University Press.

Carter, Claire. 1991. "Whatever Ought to Be, Can Be." *Parade*
(May 12). New York: Parade Publications.

Childhood Diseases on the Rise. 1988. *Seattle Times* (January
3). Reprinted from *The Washington Post.*

Chopra, Deepak, MD. 1994. *Journey into Healing.* N.p.:
Harmony Books.

Classroom of Babel. 1991. *Newsweek* (Feb. 11).

Clinton, Hillary. 1996. *It Takes a Village.* New York: Simon &
Schuster.

Coles, Robert. 1986. *Children in Crisis.* New York: Harper &
Row.

Collins, Marva, and Civia Tamarkin. 1982. *Marva Collins' Way.*
Boston: Houghton Mifflin.

Counselor, The 14, no. 1 (January/February 1996). Arlington,
Va.: National Association of Alcoholism and Drug Abuse
Counselors.

___ 14, no. 2 (March/April 1996). Arlington, Va.: National
Association of Alcoholism and Drug Abuse Counselors.

Covey, Stephen R. 1989. *The Seven Habits of Highly Effective
People.* New York: Simon & Schuster.

___. 1991. *Principle-Centered Leadership.* New York: Summit
Books.

___. 1994. *First Things First.* New York: Simon & Schuster.

de Chardin, Pierre Telhard. *Future of Man.* New York: Harper
& Row Publishing Co.

De Pree, Max. 1989. *Leadership Is an Art.* New York: Dell
Publishing.

DeWitt, Virginia. 1995. "Generation X: Implications for
Treatment." *The Counselor* 13, no. 6 (November/
December): 21-23. Arlington, Va.: National Association

of Alcoholism and Drug Abuse Counselors.

Dole, Bob. 1996. "We Must Make America Safe Again." *Family Circle* (July 16): 132. New York: USA Publishing.

Dorris, Michael. 1989. *The Broken Cord.* New York: Harper & Row.

Douglass, Frederick. 1845. *Narration of the Life of Frederick Douglass.* Garden City, N.Y.: Doubleday & Co.

Farber, Barry. 1991. *Crisis in Education.* San Francisco: Jossey-Bass.

Farber, Jerry. 1970. *The Student as a Nigger.* New York: Pocket Books.

Finn, Chester E., Jr. 1991. *We Must Take Charge.* New York: The Free Press.

Friedan, Betty. 1987. *Second Stage.* New York: Summit Books.

Garbarino, J., N. Dubrow, and K. Kostelny. 1992. *Children in Danger.* San Francisco: Jossey-Bass.

Garreau, Joel. 1991. *Edge City.* New York: Doubleday.

Geyer, Georgia Anne. 1990. "The Concept of Community May Be Making a Comeback." *Seattle Times* (September 2).

Gibbs, Nancy. "How Should We Teach Our Kids about Sex?" *Time:* 60-65. New York: Time Inc.

Goodall, Jane. 1990. *Through a Window.* Boston: Houghton-Mifflin Co.

Gordon, Susan. 1989. "America's Day Care Crisis." *Parents* (March). New York: USA Publishing.

Gordon, Thomas. 1980. *Leadership Effectiveness Training.* L.E.T. New York: Bantam Books.

Gravelle, Karen, and Leslie Peterson. 1992. *Teenage Fathers.* Englewood Cliffs: J. Messner.

Gregory, Dick, with Robert Lipsyte. 1964. *Nigger.* New York: Pocket Books.

Griffin, Mary, M.D. 1983. *A Cry for Help.* New York: Doubleday.

Griffin, Susan. 1996. "Can Imagination Save Us?" *Utne Reader* (July-August): 43-46. Minneapolis: LENS Publishing Co. Inc.

Gross, Ronald and Beatrice. 1985. *The Great School Debate.* New York: Simon & Schuster, Inc.

Hafen, Brent Q., and Kathryn J. Frandsen. 1986. *Youth Suicide.* Evergreen, Col.: Cordillera Press.

Havel, Vaclav. 1985. "Politics, Morality, and Civility." *The Graywolf Annual*: 9-27. St. Paul, Minn.: Graywolf Press.

Hevly, Nancy. 1988. "Children in Poor Hands." *Seattle Times* (January 3).

Hopfensperger, Jean. 1996. "Eurowelfare." *Star Tribune* (April 15, 16, 17). Minneapolis.

"How Much Does Depression Cost Society?" 1994. *The Harvard Mental Health Letter* 11, no. 4 (October). Boston: Harvard Medical School Health Publications Group.

Hull, Jon D. 1993. "A Boy and His Gun." *Time* (Aug. 2): 21-27. New York: Time Inc.

Jacobs, Jane. 1961. *The Death and Life of Great American Cities.* New York: Random House.

Jennings, Peter. 1995. *Children First—Real Solutions.* ABC television documentary (April 20).

Johnson, Eric W. 1984. *Raising Children to Achieve.* New York: Walker & Company.

Kagen, Jerome. 1984. *The Nature of the Child.* New York: Basic Books.

Kahn, Herman. 1978. *The Next 200 Years.* London: Sphere Books, Ltd.

Kemmis, Stephen, and Robin McTaggart, eds. 1988. *The Action Research Planner* (3d ed.). Victoria, Canada: Deakin University.

Kiplinger, Austin H., and Knight A. Kiplinger. 1989. *America in the Global '90s.* Washington, D.C.: Kiplinger Books.

Kohl, Herbert. 1978. *Growing with Your Children.* Boston: Little, Brown & Co.

Landau, Elaine. 1990. *Child Abuse.* Rev. ed. Englewood Cliffs: J. Messner.

Lemann, Nicholas. 1991. *The Promised Land.* New York: Alfred Knopf.

References

"Literary Gap." 1988. *Time* (December 19). New York: Time Inc.

MacKendrick, Paul, and Herbert M. Howe, eds. 1952. *Classics in Translation*. Madison: The University of Wisconsin Press.

McLennan, Roy. 1980. *Managing Organizational Change*. Englewood Cliffs, N.J.: Prentice-Hall, Inc.

"Mental Illness in the US." 1966. *The Therapist Report* 9, no. 2 (May). Ormond Beach, Fla.: American Association of Behavioral Therapists.

Miller, Jo Ann, and Susan Weissman. 1986. *The Parent's Guide to Daycare*. New York: Bantam Books.

Moynihan, Daniel Patrick. 1986. *Family and Nation*. New York: Harcourt Brace Jovanovich Publishers.

Mumford, Lewis. 1934. *Technics and Civilization*. New York: Harcourt, Brace and Company.

Naisbitt, John. 1982. *Megatrends*. New York: Warner Brothers..

Naisbitt, John, and Patricia Aburdene. 1990. *Megatrends* 2000. New York: William Morrow and Company, Inc.

Packard, Vance. 1983. *Our Endangered Children*. Boston: Little, Brown & Co.

Peters, Thomas J., and Robert H. Waterman, Jr. 1982. *In Search of Excellence*. New York: Harper and Row.

Pines, Burton Gale. 1982. *Back to Basics*. New York: Morrow.

Restak, Richard M., M.D. 1986. *The Infant Mind*. New York: Doubleday.

Robertson, Ian. 1987. *Sociology*. 3d ed. New York: Worth Publishers, Inc.

Spencer, Paula. 1996. "Growing Pains." *Woman's Day* (July 16, 67-70. New York: Hachette Filipacchi Magazines, Inc.

Stampp, Kenneth M. 1956. *The Peculiar Institution*. New York: Random House.

Storer, John H. 1968. *Man in the Web of Life*. New York: Signet Books.

1991 World Almanac, The. Boston: Houghton Mifflin Co.

World Almanac and the Book of Facts 1988, The. New York: Scripps

Howard Co.

World Almanac and the Book of Facts 1991, The. New York: Scripps Howard Co.

Toffler, Alvin. 1981. *The Third Wave.* New York: Bantam Books, Inc.

Toufexis, Anstasia, Mary Cronin, Melissa Ludtke, and James Willwerth. 1991. "Innocent Victims." *Time* (May 13). New York: Time Inc.

US Department of Labor. 1983. *Time of Change: 1983 Handbook of Women Workers.* Bulletin 298. Washington D.C.: U.S. Dept. of Labor, Office of the Secretary of Women's Bureau, Washington, D.C.

Wallis, Claudia. 1994. "A Class of Their Own." *Time* (Oct. 31). New York: Time Inc.

Washington, Booker T. 1968. *Up from Slavery.* New York: Magnum Books.

White, Burton L. 1975. *The First Three Years of Life.* Englewood Cliffs, N.J.: Prentice-Hall, Inc.

Williams, Terry Tempest. 1985. *White Pelicans. The Graywolf Annual.* St. Paul, Minn.: Graywolf Press.

Wilson, John Oliver. 1986. *After Affluence.* New York: William Murrow & Co.

Wright, John W., ed. 1995. *The Universal Almanac 1996.* Kansas City Mo.: Andrews and McMeel.

Yapko, Michael D. 1994. *Suggestions of Abuse.* New York: Simon & Schuster.

Zigler, Edward. 1994. "Early Intervention to Prevent Juvenile Delinquency." *The Harvard Mental Health Letter* 11, no. 3 (September): 5-7. Boston: Harvard Medical School Health Publications Group.

Index

≈‡ ‡≈